"Very few writers (or broadcasters for that matter) know the rules of the games they cover as Hal Lebovitz did. His precise and encyclopedic knowledge of that single aspect alone made him an invaluable resource. But beyond that, Hal was a skillful and insightful writer with a fine blend of enthusiasm, empathy and, when warranted, a critical eye. To top it all off, Hal was a mensch. It was a pleasure to know him and to learn from him." — **BOB COSTAS**

HAL LEBOVITZ was inducted into the writers' wing of the Baseball Hall of Fame in 2000. For six decades (1942–2005) he reported on practically every notable sports event with honest words and firmly held opinions. He got his first job covering high school sports for the *Cleveland News* in 1942 and soon became a beat writer covering the Cleveland Browns and Cleveland Indians. He was hired by the *Plain Dealer* in 1960 and was that paper's sports editor from 1964 to 1982. He was also a regular contributor to the *Sporting News* from 1947 to 1993. His popular column "Ask Hal, the Referee" ran from 1959 through 2005 and was syndicated nationally for many years. His stories appeared in *Sport* magazine, the *Saturday Evening Post, Collier's,* and many other publications. His writing was featured 17 times in the annual *Best Sports Stories* and was selected for numerous other anthologies. He won countless writing awards and was inducted into 12 halls of fame. A former high school and college athlete, he coached baseball, basketball, and football and officiated all three sports. He umpired area baseball and softball games as a member of the Cleveland Umpires Association, worked as a referee in the National Basketball League (the forerunner of the National Basketball Association), and once traveled around the country with the Harlem Globetrotters, refereeing their games against college all-stars. A collection of his sportswriting, *The Best of Hal Lebovitz,* was published in 2004. He continued to write regularly for the *News-Herald* (Lake County, Ohio) and the *Morning Journal* (Lorain, Ohio) until just a few weeks before his death in October, 2005.

D1432302

Ask Hal

Answers to Fans'
Most Interesting Questions
about Baseball Rules
from a Hall-of-Fame Sportswriter

Hal Lebovitz

GRAY & COMPANY, PUBLISHERS
CLEVELAND

*This book is dedicated to my team—my beloved bride, Margie,
and my son, Neil, and daughter, Lynn—and to my dear friends
and co-workers who supported me along the way.*

Editors: Neil Lebovitz, Les Levine, Eric Broder

Gray & Company, Publishers
www.grayco.com

Library of Congress Cataloging-in-Publication Data

Lebovitz, Hal.
Ask Hal : answers to fans' most interesting questions about
baseball rules from a hall-of-fame sportswriter / Hal Lebovitz.
p. cm.
ISBN-13: 978-1-59851-034-8 (pbk.)
1. Baseball—Rules. 2. Baseball—Miscellanea. 3. Baseball—
History. I. Title.
GV877.L33 2007
796.35702'022—dc22

Printed in the United States of America
10 9 8 7 6 5 4 3 2 1

Contents

Foreword

I was an eleven-year-old shortstop playing for the undefeated Red Sox of the South Euclid, Ohio, Little League. The Tigers had the tying run on first base with one out late in the game.

The batter hit a gapper to right center field that figured to at least tie the game. Our right fielder chased the ball down and (on several bounces) got it to me, in perfect cut-off position, as the runner from first rounded third and the batter headed for a triple.

Where was the play? The decision was made for me. Out of the corner of my eye, I saw that the potential tying run had tripped and fallen, and now both runners were heading toward third base from different directions.

I joined the race toward the bag. With both Tigers firmly standing on third base, I tagged each of them, thinking that somehow I had just invented an inning-ending double play.

Common sense dictated otherwise. The umpire, coaches, and fans in the stands knew that only one out should be recorded, but they could only guess which runner should go back to the bench.

One thing they all agreed: they should Ask Hal.

From the 1950s through the 1990s, scenes like that took place regularly in Northeast Ohio. It happened in Little League, sandlot, softball, high school, and even the pros. The more bizarre the play, the more likely someone—fans, players, umpires—needed a second opinion.

It even happened in World Series games. And when it did, the phone would ring at Hal Lebovitz's modest home in University Heights, Ohio. Hal took those calls, of course, from the NBC broadcasters phoning urgently during the game, between innings, to verify if the right call had been made on the field.

How did Hal Lebovitz become known as one of the foremost experts in baseball rules?

For more than forty years, Hal answered questions about the rules from everybody and anybody who wrote to him. He started his "Ask Hal" column at the old *Cleveland News*. Its popularity was one reason the *Plain Dealer* hired him when the *News* folded—and why the *Sport-*

ing News carried the column nationally for decades. Hal continued answering readers' questions—later for both the *News Herald* and *Lorain Journal*—until shortly before his death in 2005.

Hal would answer questions about any sport. But baseball drew the most questions. Often the most interesting ones, too. And unlike most other sports, which change their rules frequently, baseball has changed its rules seldom since 1901. (Other than changing the height of the pitcher's mound, and the designated hitter "experiment," they got it right.) That's why Hal's answers about baseball still make for such great reading today.

While reviewing thousands of "Ask Hal" clippings from forty years for this collection, I was amazed at how the same situations kept popping up from one decade to the next, with only the names of the participants changing. Carlos Baerga did the same thing in the 1990s that Minnie Minoso did in the '50s.

That's the beauty of the game of baseball, and that's why "Ask Hal" is still relevant today. Baseball seems like a simple game, but it is really the most complex. And the umpire always gets the final say.

It has been said that no matter how many games you watch or take part in, something will always happen that you've never seen before. That was true for generations of fans in Northeast Ohio, and lucky for them, Hal was there to explain what they saw.

This book collects many of Hal's readers' most interesting questions—and Hal's sharpest answers—from those four decades. They're organized loosely into ten chapters, but their sequence is much the same as the way Hal received them from readers: at random. Flip through and stop on any page and you'll find a question that might spark a lively debate at any dinner table, or an answer that will settle a bet at the local tavern. This is no encyclopedia. It's meant for fun reading. Skip around. Dip into the pages. Find a gem, and share it with a family member or coworker. Then sit back and listen as they remember a situation of their own that called for an answer from Ask Hal. It's probably in here, too.

— Les Levine

(Les Levine has covered sports on radio and television in Northeast Ohio since 1972. His TV program featured Hal Lebovitz as a weekly guest for ten years. Les is also the lead Sunday sports columnist for the News-Herald *and* Lorain Journal, *a position previously held by Hal.)*

Ask Hal

1

Baseball Basics

·················· **10 WAYS TO REACH** ··················

Q: While we were sitting in a local bar one night a representative of the Atlanta Braves walked in. Naturally, the tide of conversation shifted to baseball. He then set everyone's mind spinning with the statement that there are 10 ways of reaching first base. We could not come up with 10. Can you? *—Jeff E. Boy, Lewisburg, PA* [9/2/77]

A: Try these on for size: You can reach first: 1) on an error; 2) by being hit by a pitched ball; 3) by interference by the catcher or a fielder; 4) on a fielder's choice; 5) a base on balls; 6) a base hit; 7) a dropped third strike by a catcher; 8) a batted ball which hits a base runner; 9) a batted ball which hits the base umpire before passing a fielder; 10) as a pinch runner.

At least you discovered one way to get your mind spinning in a bar without buying a drink.

·················· **BRINGING HOME A RUN** ··················

Q: How many ways are there to bring home a run? *—J. R. C., Coshocton, OH* [4/10/75]

A: Of course a home run will do it. Also any kind of base hit that would move a teammate far enough to score. The other ways (assuming there is a man on third): stolen base, sacrifice bunt, sacrifice fly, catcher's interference with the bases loaded, obstruction, hit batsman (also with the bases loaded, wild pitch, passed ball, force play, fielder's choice, including a double play or triple play which isn't a force) error, balk, base on balls with the sacks loaded, dropped third strike when play is made on batter going to first, and a ground rule on an overthrow which would send the runner home.

That's 17. Can anybody think of any others?

······················· **HIT-AND-RUN** ·······················

Q: What's the difference between the hit-and-run term in baseball and the run-and-hit? I say there is no such thing as a run-and-hit. —*Glenn Morris, Sharpsville, PA* [6/9/70]

A: It's just the reverse. There really is no such thing as the hit-and-run. Whenever this term is used it really means run-and-hit. The purpose is to break up a possible double play and/or to get the runner an extra base. The runner doesn't wait until the ball is hit. He runs with the pitch because he knows the batter is going to try to hit. The batter attempts to hit behind the runner when the play is on. But even if he doesn't, it's as good as a sacrifice *if* he can hit it on the ground.

So, every time you hear the expression "hit-and-run," switch it around in your mind. It means run-and-hit.

······················· **THE WINNING RUN** ·······················

Q: What is the definition of a "winning run" in baseball? Example: The Indians are playing the Yankees. The Indians score one run in the first inning and another in the sixth. The Yankees score once in the seventh and the Indians win, 2-1. Say Wayne Garland works the first five innings and gets credit for the victory. Would that mean the first run was the winning run, or would the run scored in the sixth be the winner? My co-workers say the sixth-inning run is the winning run, but in that case why wouldn't the reliever get credit for the victory? Twenty rides on your answer. —*Name withheld by request* [11/23/77]

A: The rules book defines the winning pitcher as the pitcher of record—assuming he has gone at least five innings if he's the starter—when his team goes ahead and never loses the lead. Therefore, Garland has to be the winner in your example.

There is no official definition for "winning run," but teams do keep this statistic for their own private records. In almost every case major league statisticians consider the winning run to be the one that puts the team ahead to stay. Since the run in the first inning put the Indians ahead and since they never were tied, that run is considered the winning run in your case, which makes you a winner.

WHO IS RIGHT?

Q: Please settle this argument: There is a runner on first and the batter hits the ball to the first baseman. He steps on first, then throws to the second baseman who steps on second. The fielding team claims it is a double play but the offensive team says the runner had to be tagged because the force is off. Who is right? —*D. K., Rocky River, OH* [6/3/75]

A: The offensive team is right. When first base was touched that base became unoccupied and, therefore, the force was off. The runner going to second on such a play *must* be tagged in order to complete the double play.

I'm assuming you didn't have an umpire because that's what he would have said, too. Otherwise he would have been wrong.

FAIR OR FOUL?

Q: What is the ruling in baseball regarding a ground ball that bounces along the line in fair territory, then bounces over the bag and comes down in foul territory? I say foul. Others I've talked to say fair. Who's right? —*Kim Haughawout, Monroeville, OH* [8/19/79]

A: You yelled "foul" too soon. It's a fair ball, for it passed over the bag in fair territory.

DESIGNATED HITTER

Q: Why does the American League use the designated hitter and the National League doesn't? —*Steve Payton, Mount Gilead, OH* [8/4/90]

A: In 1973 the American League, believing it needed something to spark fan interest, voted to try the designated hitter as an experiment for three years. The National League owners said it would watch with interest. The American League liked it so much that after two years (1975) they adopted the designated hitter rule on a permanent basis. The National League, doing exceedingly well without what it considered a "gimmick" voted against the DH. It's been that way ever since, which is ridiculous. There should be conformity. To date, the respective league commissioners have been too chicken to decide the debate: DH or no DH?

IS IT AN ERROR?

Q: A disagreement has arisen over what is an error and what isn't. I believe when the player, in the official scorer's judgment, misplays a ball that he considers should have been caught it doesn't have to be touched to be scored an error. My opponents argue that if a player lets a routine fly fall at his feet and doesn't touch it, it isn't an error. They argue it's a mental error and mental errors are not scored as errors in the book. I consider this ridiculous and illogical. Please help us clear this up. —*Tim Hildebrand, Euclid, OH* [8/3/89]

A: A player does not have to touch a ball to be charged with an error. If, in the judgment of the scorer, the ball should have been caught with ordinary effort he must rule it an error.

HIT OR ERROR?

Q: A batter hits a routine ground ball to the third baseman. The ball goes right through the fielder's legs, without touching his glove, although he did put his glove down. Should this be scored a hit or an error? What about a hard hit ball that goes right through his legs without touching his glove? This type of scoring is hard for me. —*Mike Flanagan, Brecksville, OH* [4/7/75]

A: This play is relatively easy for the official scorer. When a ball goes through a fielder's legs call it an error and you'll be right at least 95 percent of the time. As a matter of fact, you're always right, because scoring is a matter of judgment and whatever you call is right.

When a fielder is in front of a ball he should be able to catch it or knock it down. If he doesn't do either, he didn't accomplish what he was supposed to do—hence the error. Only if the ball is going a zillion miles an hour or takes a horrendous bounce would I give the fielder the benefit of doubt if the ball goes through his legs.

Here's the simple rule of thumb: If the batter is safe on a ball that should have been fielded with ordinary effort, call it an error. The emphasis is on the words ordinary effort.

But don't worry about your calls. Call 'em as you see 'em and ignore the critics. They're always there.

Out of Left Field

Q: I have been around baseball a long time but never heard of this play. I have asked umpires and former players and the answers are about 50-50. This is the play: A pitcher grabs a grounder between home and first. He tries to throw the ball to first base but can't get the ball out of the web of his glove. So he takes off his glove and tosses the glove *with the ball in it*, to the first baseman before the runner reaches the bag. The first baseman catches the glove with the ball in it. Is the runner out or safe? —*Andrew Tablack, Campbell, OH* [10/23/64]

A: Pardon my glove, sir. The runner is *out*.

WILD PITCH: AN ERROR?

Q: Is a wild pitch classified as an error? If a run scores on a wild pitch that otherwise wouldn't have scored, is it earned or unearned? —*Mark A. Miller, Sugarcreek, OH* [12/12/83]

A: A wild pitch, just as a passed ball, is not listed as an error. Both are in their own categories. If a run scores because of a wild pitch, it's an earned run because the pitcher was responsible for it. An earned run is one the pitcher gave up, not necessarily one the opponents earned.

PASSED BALL

Q: I claim a passed ball is officially recorded as an error on the catcher. My friend claims it isn't. Who's right? —*Chris Robbins, Dover, OH* [10/11/90]

A: Your friend. Because the catcher and pitcher are involved in so many pitches, passed balls and wild pitches have their own respective categories, rather than being scored as errors.

··············· GETTING THE WIN ···············

Q: In professional baseball, how long does a pitcher who starts a game have to work in order to get a win? —*Wayne E. Brewer, Sheffield Lake, OH* [7/10/77]

A: A starting pitcher *must* pitch at least five *full* innings to be credited with a victory for any game that goes six innings or more. If it's a completed five-inning game, the starter must go at least four innings.

And, of course, his team must win.

··············· RECORDING A SAVE ···············

Q: Could you please tell me how a pitcher records a save? —*Tim McNulty, Mayfield Heights, OH* [8/8/85]

A: First, he must finish the game won by his club and he is *not* the winning pitcher. Then he must qualify under one of the following conditions: (a) he pitches for at least three innings, or (b) he enters the game with a lead of no more than three runs and pitches for at least one inning, or (c) he enters the game with the potential tying run already on base, at bat or in the on-deck circle. If he can't satisfy one of these options, he doesn't deserve a save.

··············· EARNED RUN AVERAGE ···············

Q: How do you determine a pitcher's earned run average? —*Doug Hanson, Shaker Heights, OH* [7/20/75]

A: If your league plays nine-inning games multiply the number of earned runs the pitcher has allowed by 9. Divide the product by the number of innings he has pitched.

If you have a pocket calculator, it's easy. If you haven't, I hope you know your multiplication tables.

··············· TAGGING UP ···············

Q: Would you please settle this bet? A friend says a base runner must tag up to the base on every pitch? I say no. Who is correct? —*David Mahon, Middleburg Heights, OH* [8/17/75]

A: You are. Collect.

DOES THE RUN COUNT?

Q: There are two outs and a runner is on third base. Batter swings and misses the third strike which the catcher drops. The runner from third touches home plate before the batter is put out at first base. Does the run count? —*John Sullivan, Shaker Heights, OH* [9/23/83]

A: No. A run never can count when the third out is made by the batter before he reaches first base.

INFIELD FLY RULE

Q: Could you please explain the infield fly rule in baseball? I can't seem to get it straight. —*David Shaub, Akron, OH* [12/16/80]

A: An infield fly is a fair fly ball—this does not include a line drive or an attempted bunt that goes into the air—which can be caught by an infielder with ordinary effort when first and second are occupied or the bases are loaded before there are two outs. When the umpire calls "infield fly," the batter is automatically out and the runners can try to advance, if they wish, at their own risk.

Remember, there must be fewer than two outs, at least first and second must be occupied, and the fly must be the kind an infielder can catch with ordinary effort. The pitcher and catcher and anybody who stations himself, or herself, in the infield area are considered infielders on such flies.

There, I don't think I left anything out.

Out of Left Field

Q: Runner on first base, two outs and the home team is losing, 2-1, bottom of the ninth. The batter hits a home run. The runner on first stops at second and waits for the batter to congratulate him. They then run to third base side by side but the man who hit the home run touches third before his teammate does. Does the home team win or lose? —*Mickey McHugh, Lorain, OH* [6/20/90]

A: The home team loses. The batter was out the instant he passed the preceding runner, and when he tagged third before his teammate he became the third out, ending the inning immediately—and the game. The moral to your play? Don't be in a hurry to party.

·················· **THE EDGE OF HOME PLATE** ··················

Q: I keep getting different answers to this question. Is the black edge of home plate part of the actual plate and, therefore, part of the strike zone? Or is it just the outline framing the plate? Is the rule different in softball? Finally, are there regulations regarding the width of the black? —*Duncan Holoday, Cleveland, OH* [1/8/87]

A: The black is just a border. It has nothing to do with home plate and it isn't even a requirement. Only the white counts. The white slab has a 17-inch front that faces the pitcher, and the pitch has to be over some part of the white in order to be a strike. The plates in softball and baseball are identical. The black border, when there is one, has no size limit. It can be so wide it touches the batter's box and sometimes I wish a team would install a border that large to make the radio and TV announcers realize how wrong they are—and how silly—when they say, "That strike just got the black," or "The pitcher is playing the black perfectly today." Once more, the black is not part of the plate. And a pitch is not a strike if it only goes over the black.

·················· **ERRORS CAN'T HELP** ··················

Q: Recently you answered a question on how to figure "on base percentage." I can't believe you don't consider reaching first on an error. Reaching any base on an error should credit the batter with an on-base effort. —*Ken Labus, Mayfield Village, OH* [5/3/91]

A: I can't believe you think that. Why expand a batter's on-base percentage when he got there through no ability of his own? When he reaches on an error it's a pure gift and it shouldn't raise his average. The answer given was correct. Reaching base on an error doesn't pad a batter's on-base average. He would have made an out, except for the error, and that's how it's figured.

SLUGGING PERCENTAGE

Q: How do you figure slugging percentage? —*Mark Kiessling, Warren, OH* [7/1/89]

A: It's figured the same as batting average, except that each hit is worth the total bases the batter gets on the hit. Example: Suppose a batter is up 10 times and gets four hits. Two of those hits are singles, one is a double, and one is a home run. That's a total of eight bases. Divide his number of at bats (10) into his total bases (8) and you get his slugging percentage. It comes to .800 in this case, which is exceptional.

HIT BY PITCH RBI

Q: In a game against the Royals, the Yankees have the bases loaded and Don Baylor is up. He was hit by a pitch. The official scorer ruled it an RBI. Can you explain why? —*Michael Long, New Philadelphia, OH* [8/8/85]

A: He gets the RBI because he forced in the run. He would get it if he walked, also. In other words, the run was scored by the batter, not by any error. Hence, an RBI for him.

FIGURING GAMES BEHIND

Q: How do you figure "games behind"? Is it the same for "games behind" in the wild-card chase? —*Jane Lindamood, Oberlin, OH* [8/19/00]

A: To determine how many games one team is behind another, whether it's behind the leader of the division or behind another team—as in the wild-card race—subtract the number of victories the team has from the number of victories the leading team has. Then do the same with the number of losses each has. Add these two numbers together and divide the sum by 2. The result is the games behind figure. Example: Last Tuesday morning, the White Sox had won 70 games and lost 48. The Indians had won 61 and lost 54. The difference in the victory column was 9 and the difference in the loss column was 6. Add 9 and 6. The sum is 15. Divide by 2. Result: 7½. The Indians were 7½ games behind the White Sox. On that day, the leading wild-card team was Oakland, with 63 victories and 54 losses.

Thus, the A's were two games ahead of the Indians in the victory column and they were even in the loss column. Sum: 2. Divide by 2. Result: 1. The Indians were one game behind Oakland.

THE MAGIC NUMBER

Q: How do you figure a team's magic number? —*Daniel Langston, Mansfield, OH* [6/21/89]

A: Determine the number of games remaining for that team. Add one. From this total subtract the number of games the team is ahead in the "Lost" column from the club below it. Example: Suppose the Indians are in first place, with 10 games remaining and they are three games ahead of the second-place Orioles. Add 1 to 10. The sum is 11. Now subtract 3 from that total and the Indians' magic number is 8. This means that any combination of Indians victories and Orioles losses that add up to 8 would give the Tribe the pennant. If the Indians won three of their remaining games and the Orioles lost five, the Tribe would finish on top.

DEFENSIVE INDIFFERENCE

Q: In a Chicago Cubs game I saw on TV, with the score tied in the bottom of the ninth, Cubs at bat, two outs, runners at first and third, Leon Durham apparently steals second base to eliminate the possible force play there. However, because the opposition didn't hold him on and failed to attempt a throw, it was ruled a no stolen base. I never heard of this. Is it correct? It seems illogical to me. I think Durham should be credited with a stolen base. Please enlighten. —*Bruce Helmer, Mansfield, OH* [8/24/88]

A: Here's the rule: "No stolen base shall be scored when a runner advances solely because of the defensive team's indifference to his advance. Score it a fielder's choice." The opposing team was concerned only with the runner on third, for he represented the winning run. It wasn't going to chance a throw to second which might allow that run to score. So it treated Durham with "indifference." Hence, he didn't steal second. It was given to him.

HIT THE SHOWER

Q: If a pro baseball player started a game, but after three innings the manager took him out, would it be possible for that player to go back in three innings later at a different position? I say he can go back as long as he remains in his original batting spot. Five dollars says I'm right. —G. M., *Broadview Heights, OH* [6/12/77]

A: You never were more wrong. Once a player is removed from the game he's through for the remainder of the game. He can take his shower. And you just took a bath—for five bucks.

Out of Left Field

Q: I play in the Cleveland 3A Softball League. With two outs and our team trailing, 10-1 in the fifth inning, the rain was getting heavier. Intentionally, I proceeded to foul off pitches in hopes of prolonging the game to an unofficial standoff. The umpire then called time, saying that if I foul off one more pitch he would call me out. Can he make that ruling legally? —*Karl Genda, Strongsville, OH* [6/8/75]

A: No, but he can do worse. He can forfeit the game because, as you admit, you were intentionally delaying the game. In this case, the results would be the same.

   You must be a wizard with the bat. I presume you're hitting 1.000.

SAFE SPOTS

Q: Is the base a safety spot for the runner? In other words, say a runner is hit by a batted ball while standing on the base. Is he or isn't he out? Also, is the ball still in play? —*Adam Abelha, Cleveland, OH* [10/15/83]

A: In baseball, the base is *not* a safe haven. The runner is out when hit by a batted ball that has not been touched by an infielder and the batter is awarded first base. The only exception is on an infield fly. In this case the batter is automatically out and the runner is safe if the fly hits him while he is on the bag. In all cases the ball is dead the instant it hits the runner.

   In softball, the base *is* a safe spot. If the runner is hit by the ball while standing on the bag he is *not* out. But the ball is dead and the batter gets first base. Keep your eye on the ball.

TRIPS TO THE MOUND

Q: Please settle this disagreement I had with a lieutenant where I work. I claim an American League manager is limited to two trips to the mound in *each inning* and the lieutenant claims a manager can only talk to his pitcher two times per *game* before a relief pitcher must be brought in. A small wager rides on your answer. [2/15/77]

A: A manager is permitted *one* trip to the mound per inning. The second trip in the same *inning* means the pitcher must be removed.

Once upon a time the rules made it two trips per *game*, and out, but it was cut to *inning* several years ago. The lieutenant must have been out marching.

WAYS TO SACRIFICE

Q: For the batter to be credited with a sacrifice fly, doesn't a run have to score? For a sacrifice to be credited, doesn't the batter have to bunt? —*Glenn Worley, Parma, OH* [7/20/75]

A: There are two kinds of sacrifices: the sacrifice fly and the sacrifice bunt. In order to receive credit for a sacrifice fly, the batter *must* score a run. For the batter to be credited with a sacrifice bunt, he must bunt.

SQUEEZE PLAYS

Q: Because there was confusion last year between managers and umpires, I would like to know the difference between the regular squeeze play and the suicide squeeze? Doesn't the batter have to swing the bat to make it a suicide squeeze? —*Randall J. Daniels* [4/3/70]

A: On a "suicide squeeze" the runner from third breaks with the pitcher's motion toward the plate. On the regular squeeze, better known as the "safety squeeze," the runner gets a good lead but delays his break for home until the ball actually is bunted.

On the "suicide squeeze" the runner must be careful not

to break too soon. If he does, he gives the play away and the pitcher will throw for the batter's head, forcing him to step out of the way so the catcher can make the tag. If the batter doesn't duck it could be suicide, although this is not the reason the play is so named. If the runner is off with the pitch and the batter misses the bunt it's suicide for the runner. He becomes an easy out, hence the name.

In neither type of squeeze does the batter swing away. He squares up and tries to bunt. If he did swing while the runner was coming in, that really could be suicide.

ON THE RECORD

Q: Here is a simple question that has brought about some controversy in the office. If a major league game is called because of rain after five full innings with the score tied, isn't that game put into the record books for batting, pitching, and fielding records? I contend that it goes down as a game played even though it will be rescheduled later. Is this a correct contention? —*Michael P. Shearer, Cleveland, OH* [7/20/77]

A: I support your contention, for you are 100 percent correct.

BANJO HITTER

Q: What is a banjo hitter? —*Buddy Clifton, Painesville, OH* [9/30/75]

A: A banjo hitter is one who has little power, who hits the ball as if he were hitting it with a hollow banjo rather than a solid bat. I'm glad you didn't ask me who.

WHY A "K"?

Q: I am 10 and I'm a pitcher on the Little League team. Every time I strike out a batter, my coach puts a "K" in the scorebook. No one knows why a "K" stands for strikeout. Do you? —*Jacob Jakubick, Mansfield, OH* [8/4/90]

A: Research indicates it came about this way: Since the letter "S" could be interpreted as a sacrifice, it wasn't advisable to use it for a strikeout, too. In the early days, the umpires would shout "Strike" loudly, with accent on the "K," making it sound, "stri-K-u." Hence, the first scorers considered the "K" a perfect symbol for identifying a strikeout and it became common practice. Actually, there is nothing official about it. A scorer can use any shorthand he desires. Just so he is able to reconstruct the game from his scorebook whenever the occasion arises. I hope you have many, many "K's" as your pitching career continues.

························· **GROUNDOUT RBI** ·······················

Q: Please settle this: Bases loaded, one out. Batter ducks away from pitch. Ball hits bat and rolls between mound and the plate. Both pitcher and catcher go for the ball. Runner is thrown out at first. One run scores. Is this scored as a sacrifice, fielder's choice, or just a routine groundout, with an RBI? —*N. Landolfi, Ashtabula, OH* [5/26/71]

A: The scoring is basic: the batter grounds out and gets an RBI. Actually, the bat deserves the RBI. The batter merely attached to it.

····················· **EARNED OR UNEARNED?** ··················

Q: If the pitcher walks the first four men, is the run earned or unearned? —*C. K., Garfield Heights, OH* [5/7/59]

A: The run may be a gift, but the pitcher did the giving, so he's charged with an earned run.

····················· **EXACT MEASUREMENTS** ··················

Q: It is 99 feet from home to first base. We all agree that it is from the back corner of home plate, but is it to the front, middle, or back of first base? —*Harvey Cohen* [6/29/75]

A: It's from the rear point of home plate to the front edge of the base—exactly 90 feet. As you get older it seems longer.

····················· **WIDTH OF HOME PLATE** ··················

Q: My daughter's school had a trivia question, "What is the width of home plate?" I took my daughter to the library and found a book called *Baseball for Everyone*, published in 1948. According to that book, home plate is 12 inches wide. But home plate is now 17 inches wide. We went back to the library to find out when it was changed, but only could find out that home plate once was round, then went to square, and then went to five sides that we have now. When did the size change from 12 inches to 17? —*Tereasa Carpenter, Marion, OH* [10/1/84]

A: Home plate may have been round initially, but almost immediately was changed to a 12-inch square and placed in the ground so that one point of the square faced the pitcher. In 1900 the front portion was filled in by drawing a line parallel to the pitcher's rubber, tangent to the point facing the rubber. This resulted in the five-sided figure with a 17-inch front width. The original 12-inch square remains inside the present figure, which is probably why the book you first looked at confused you. Geometry teachers could make this into an interesting and practical lesson.

In any event, for 84 years baseball has had the same five-sided slab with the 17-inch front that remains today's pitcher's target. It has proved a perfect plate, except to wild pitches and poor hitters.

PRONOUN TROUBLE

Q: I am a student at Watterson Lake School and me and my math teacher, Mr. Petsche, have a problem. Mr. Petsche said that if a batter in the American or National League had one or two strikes a pinch hitter could replace him. I don't think that is so. I would like to know who is right, me or Mr. Petsche.
—*John Vera* [3/9/75]

A: Your math teacher is correct. It's legal to replace a batter no matter what the count may be.

John, check out the proper use of the pronouns "I" and "me" or you may have a problem with your English teacher, too.

THE BOUNCE RULE

Q: Give me the ruling on a pitched ball that bounces before it gets to the plate: (a) if the batter swings and misses; (b) if the batter hits the ball; (c) if the batter is hit by the ball. —*Mike Hoffman, Cuyahoga Falls, OH* [7/6/75]

A: If the batter swings and misses, it's a strike. If he hits it, he'd better start running. It's the same as any other hit ball. If the ball hits him—assuming he didn't allow himself to be hit purposely—the batter would be awarded first base. A bouncing ball can hurt, too.

HOW MANY AT-BATS?

Q: How many times must a player bat in a season to have his average included in his lifetime American League batting average? —*R. G. Weinman* [10/15/63]

A: He can go to the plate only once in his lifetime and his average is in the books forever, even if it's zero.

NO-COUNT NO-HITTER

Q: If two men together would pitch a no-hitter, and the starter went 6⅔ innings and the reliever went 2⅓ innings, who would get credit for the no-hitter? —*Paul Laurie, Beachwood, OH* [6/30/63]

A: Neither one. In the no-hit department, it's nine innings or no-count.

SHORT FORFEIT

Q: Maybe this will never happen, but suppose a team such as Oakland, which was recently playing three players short, uses every available player, including pitchers, and are down to their last nine players. If one of these nine gets hurt and can't continue playing, is the game forfeited? Or can the team play a man short? —*D. H., Mentor, OH* [7/18/76]

A: The rules are specific. "A game *shall* be forfeited to the opposing team when a team is unable to field nine players." There are no "shorts" in baseball.

MAKE IT 502

Q: At the end of the season when a batter leads the league in hitting, does that include the amount of times he walks, or gets hit by a pitch, etc.? Or the amount of times he makes a plate appearance? Ted Williams, back in the 1960s, lost the title because he was walked over 200 times and did not have enough times at bat to qualify. Has the rule been changed? —*Andrew J. Lawrence, Cleveland, OH* [7/3/77]

A: Yes. The Williams case forced the change. It wasn't fair to hitters who were so dangerous that pitchers were prone to walk them. In those days, 400 official at-bats were needed to qualify for the batting title and, as you know, a walk is not a time at bat. Then a formula was established. Total plate appearances became the standard. This includes bases on balls, hit by pitcher, etc.

To qualify, a batter must make 502 plate appearances during a 162-game season. The formula: 3.1 times the number of games scheduled during the regular season. Get out your pocket calculator and you'll see it comes to 502.

DAD'S GROUND RULES

Q: My dad and I were watching a softball game and I said there was a ground-rule triple and he said there wasn't, so I bet him. Can you tell me who's right? —*John Zele, Cleveland, OH* [5/29/77]

A: Your dad. A ground-rule double is the most the book allows. Take it out of your allowance.

MENTAL ERROR?

Q: In the August 3rd game against the Rangers, runners were on first and third with one out. An easy ground ball was hit to the Indians' second baseman, who made an attempt to tag the runner coming from first base. The base runner stopped. Instead of finishing the tag, the fielder inexplicably threw to first base, even though he had no chance to get the batter, allowing the runner from first to reach second safely. To me, this was clearly an error, yet in the account of the game it was reported as a "fielder's choice." Can a fielder choose to make a bonehead play just because he fields the ball cleanly? The next batter hit a sacrifice fly to score the winning run from third, although the fly should have been the third out. The pitcher was then charged with an earned run. That run was no more earned than Frank Robinson's salary. —*Charles Gruenspan, Shaker Heights, OH* [10/3/76]

A: The play was scored properly according to the official scoring rules. There is not provision in the books for charging an error on the this type of mental misplay. If a fielder holds a ball, rather than making a throw or a tag, it's no error. That's one trouble with fielding averages. Often you don't get errors simply because you don't make the effort.

As for Robinson's salary, I'll let the Internal Revenue Service be the official scorer on that one.

SIMULATED GAME

Q: I read recently that before Tom Candiotti was pronounced fit to return to active duty, he pitched a "simulated game" on the sidelines. What does a "simulated game" mean? —*Robert Cox, Lorain, OH* [7/27/89]

A: A pitcher throws a simulated game in the bullpen. He goes to the mound there, just as he would in a game and pitches to an imaginary batter. The pitches are called and he keeps pitching until the batter walks or strikes out. He continues to do this until he retires three batters. Then he rests for about five minutes, returns to the mound, and again pitches until he retires an imaginary three batters. He does this for nine innings—if he can. If he can't, he's not ready to come off the disabled list.

WILD PITCHES, PASSED BALLS

Q: Are wild pitches and passed balls considered the same as errors in computing earned runs in a given inning? —*S. L. Mahne, Painesville, OH* [10/3/98]

A: Earned runs are runs charged against the pitcher. Since he is responsible for the wild pitch, any run resulting from that wild pitch becomes an earned run. But a passed ball is caused by the catcher, so any run resulting from the passed ball is not an earned run. It is treated the same as an error when determining earned runs.

A MIGHTY WIND

Q: This is unlikely to happen, but possible. The Cubs are playing the Mets in Chicago for the division crown. The weather conditions: sunny, with gusts of wind up to 50 miles per hour. Score: Mets 5-4 in the bottom of the ninth, two outs, one on. Jody Davis hits a screaming line drive over the shortstop. It gains height and goes over the wall and is still in the air when a strong gust brings it back to the left fielder who was watching it go. He catches it. Is Jody out or do the Cubs go on to play the winner of the other division? —*Jason Walraven, New Philadelphia, OH* [6/20/85]

A: It's an out. The Cubs are out, too, and the Mets go on. This isn't such a rare play. Not infrequently, batted balls heading for the stands are blown back into play. The ball isn't dead until it touches down beyond the playing field.

AUTOMATIC OUT

Q: I was watching a recent game between the Chicago Cubs and the Montreal Expos. The Expos' pitcher, Bryan Smith, was batting, runners on first and second. Smith tries to bunt twice and misses. Then Smith bunts again and the balls rolls foul. The ump calls him out. Is Smith out, or is it still strike two? —*Jeff Tipton, Perry, OH* [6/27/85]

A: When a batter tries to bunt after two strikes and the ball goes foul he's automatically out. You probably weren't aware of this rule because batters seldom bunt after two strikes for this very reason.

WIPED OUT – OR NOT?

Q: On August 3, Boston is at New York. After six innings of play, Boston leads the Yankees, 4-1. In the top of the seventh, Boston scores four runs. Before the Yankees get a chance to bat in the bottom of the seventh, the rains come and game is called. I thought the score reverts to 4-1 as the Boston four runs are wiped out because the Yankees *didn't go to bat in the bottom of the seventh*. This is what I thought was being done in the last 55 years of my following baseball. But behold, I see the box score and Boston wins, 8-1. Those four runs count even though the Yankees didn't get their "raps." Now I see a game between the Yankees and the Orioles in Baltimore in which the Yankees score five runs in the first half of the seventh to overcome a 3-1 deficit. Then the rains come and game reverts to the sixth and the score is 3-1 in favor of Baltimore. This time, the top of the seventh is wiped out and the other time it wasn't. How do you explain this? —*Brother Charles Zell, Monastery of the Holy Spirit, Conyers, GA* [8/20/78]

A: An incomplete inning is wiped out only when it has a bearing on the outcome of the game. In the Boston-New York game, Boston would have won whether you count the top of the incomplete inning or not. There fore, that half of the inning is included in the box score.

In the New York-Baltimore game, the top of the seventh definitely would have changed the outcome. It would have turned the Orioles, the home team, from being a winner into a loser. Therefore, the inning must be erased for the Orioles never got a chance to overcome the results of the top of the seventh.

2

At the Plate

Questions about Batting

··················· **DROPPED THIRD STRIKES** ···················

Q: Can you please explain the rule that covers when a batter may run to first base on a dropped third strike? Also, must he swing and miss? —*Michael Grella, Dover, OH* [10/13/90]

A: A third strike must be caught on the fly for the batter to be automatically out. He is also automatically out on a dropped third strike, one that touches the ground, if first base is occupied and there are fewer than two outs. When there are two outs the third strike always must be caught for the batter to be out. All third strikes, called or swinging, are treated the same under this rule.

··························· **STRIKE ZONE** ···························

Q: Is there any stated definition regarding the strike zone for a batter who assumes a crouched position? My inquiry is primarily concerned with Little League. However, if there is no definite rule for this, then perhaps the baseball rule would apply. —*Gerald D. Marks, Cleveland, OH* [7/4/70]

A: In baseball, the strike zone is the area above home plate from the batter's armpits to the top of his knees. In softball, the strike zone is a little bigger: not higher than the batter's shoulders and not lower than his knees.

But in both baseball and softball this zone is established by the umpire when the batter assumes his *natural* stance. The "natural stance" is the one the batter regularly employs and has to be one from which it is possible to take a normal swing. This rules out any of the crazy crouches designed purposely to draw a base on balls.

Thus, a crouch that's not ridiculous can be a legal, natural stance. The object is to hit the ball, not spring at it.

NO SHENANIGANS AT PLATE

Q: Can a batter position himself to allow the ball to hit him? My friends say no and I say otherwise. Obviously the reason it is rarely done is because of the risk of injury. But I say it's perfectly legal even if the batter jumps into the ball. —*Kenneth Garrison, New Mexico* [2/22/76]

A: You lose. The batter must try to avoid being hit by a pitch. If he has a chance to get out of the way and doesn't make the attempt, the pitch will be called a ball or strike by the ump, depending on the location of the ball. But the batter won't be awarded first base.

And under no condition can he jump into the ball to allow it to hit him purposely. I recall umpiring a championship game in which the home team was behind by one run in the bottom of the ninth. The bases were loaded and there were two strikes on the hitter. The next pitch was right down the middle. The batter stepped into it and proceeded to walk to first. I called "strike three" and ended the game. Let's just say the decision proved unpopular with the home fans, but consider what a travesty a game could become if such shenanigans were allowed.

FOR A COKE

Q: I have a small problem in baseball. If the batter reaches first base on an error, isn't this counted as an at-bat? My friend says the batter gets either an at-bat *and* a hit, or neither. A Coke rides on this. —*David Mahon, Middleburg Heights, OH* [6/1/75]

A: Your friend is a loser. When a batter reaches safely because of an error, he is charged with a time at bat, but not a hit.

If he accepts your victory gracefully, let your friend have a sip.

IS THE STREAK OVER?

Q: Let's say Mike Hargrove enters the game with his 21-game hitting streak intact. During the game he draws three walks and hits a sacrifice fly for no official at-bat. Is his consecutive game hitting streak still intact? —*Rick Bookman, Cleveland, OH* [5/25/80]

A: No. The sacrifice fly did him in. Had it been a sacrifice bunt or a fourth walk, or had he been hit by a pitched ball, the string would have continued. But when he hit the sacrifice fly, he was attempting to get a base hit and, since he failed, the string snapped.

ONLY RUN YOU NEED

Q: This happened to a friend of mine in a softball game: Bottom of the seventh, score 5-5, no outs, bases full. On the first pitch, my friend hits the ball way over the head of the left fielder. The field has no outfield fence. The left fielder doesn't even go after the ball and starts for the dugout. My friend trots around the bases thinking she had hit a grand slam. As she crosses the plate, the umpire informs her she will be credited with a single, one RBI, and that the final score is 6-5. I argued that since time wasn't called and that she ran all the bases, she should get a homer and four RBIs. Right? —*John Palmer, Painesville, OH* [10/24/90]

A: Wrong. Since the ball wasn't hit over a fence, the batter gets only as many bases as it takes to score the winning run. The winning run advanced from third, so your girlfriend—am I presuming correctly?—gets a single. If it's true love, you'll build a fence for her.

FLYING BATS

Q: Our protest committee must make a ruling on this: One out, man on third base. Batter hits ball to the second baseman. However, the bat splits. Both the ball and part of the bat arrive at the second baseman at approximately the same time. Second baseman fails to make the play as he moves out of the way of the bat. Umpire calls interference; batter is out and runner goes back to third. Is this a legal call or does the opposing team have a legitimate protest? —*Noel F. Mooney, Ashland, OH* [7/17/67]

A: At the All-Star game in Anaheim earlier this week I asked members of the rule committee to help you out. They say the umpire should have ignored the flying piece of bat and that the ball should have remained in play. Had the entire bat slipped from the batter's hand the umpire would have been right. But when the bat breaks and a portion goes onto the playing field it's not the batter's fault. It's simply the breaks of the game.

FOUL POLE HOMER

Q: I contend that if a well-hit ball hits the foul pole on the fly and drops foul onto the field it should be fair and the batter is entitled to make as many bases as he can. My best friend awaits your decision that it's a home run. Who is correct? —*David Vician, Cleveland, OH* [4/13/75]

A: For your friend the answer is worth waiting for. It's a home run. It would have been a home run if the foul pole hadn't been there. So why take it away from the batter?

HAMSTRUNG HOMER

Q: Joe Carter hits a home run over the fence. However, when he leaves the batter's box he severely injures his hamstring and can't circle the bases. Is he awarded a home run without touching the bases? —*Dean Brown, Dover, OH* [5/14/87]

A: When a player who has been awarded a base or bases becomes incapacitated, a substitute runner is permitted to touch the bases for him. In this case, a substitute runner would circle the bases for Carter, who would get credit for the home run. Please, let's not incapacitate Carter. Don't the Indians have enough trouble already?

IT'S A STRIKE

Q: In a recent Little League game, the batter was expecting a fast-ball, but was fooled by a changeup. As a result, the batter was way ahead of his swing and was hit on the fist by a ball. Is it a strike or does the runner get his base? —*J. P. Sammon, Bay Village, OH* [6/10/60]

A: It's a strike because he swung. Period.

CRACK SHOT

Q: Bases loaded, two outs. Batter hits the baseball and it hits one of the base runners and naturally the runner is out. What is the batter credited with, an out on a force play, a base hit, no at-bat, or exactly what? —*T. W. Hlabse, Willowick, OH* [5/18/75]

A: The batter is charged with a time at bat and is credited with a base hit. For being a crack shot, I suppose.

SMART MOVE

Q: Since a batter can run to first base on a third strike that gets away from the catcher, what's to stop a batter with two strikes from swinging at an obvious wild pitch, such as one very far outside and over the batter's head and then getting a free base? —*Buddy Clifton, Painesville, OH* [5/22/77]

A: Nothing. It's a smart move unless first base is occupied and there are fewer than two outs. In that case he shouldn't swing. He'd be automatically out—out of his mind.

COUNT STAYS

Q: Pitcher goes to full count on batter and manager makes a pitching change. Does count remain the same on the batter? I bet a friend that it does. —*Matt Battiato, Lakewood, OH* [7/26/69]

A: Collect.

CHARGED BATTER A

Q: In a high school game, Batter A is up with two outs and runners on second and third. The count is 0-2. The coach calls time and puts in Batter B as a pinch hitter for A. On the second pitch to Batter B he strikes out and the side is retired. Who is charged with the strikeout, Batter A or Batter B? —*David Abrutyn, Niles, OH* [5/20/89]

A: The strikeout is charged to Batter A. Whenever a batter is replaced after two strikes the first batter is responsible for the strikeout. Had there been one strike, Batter B would be the whiffer.

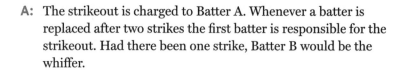

YOU'RE OUT OF ORDER

Q: I've always been puzzled by the rule involving batting-out-of-order in baseball. Suppose the proper order is Adam, Bill, and Charles. Bill singles. Then it is discovered by the defensive team that Adam is the proper batter. Before the next pitch, the defensive team appeals to the umpire. The umpire calls Adam out and tells Bill to bat again. Is this the proper ruling? —*Stephen Moyer, Lyndhurst, OH* [1/14/89]

A: Yes. When a player bats out of order, the player who was supposed to bat is out and the next batter is the one who follows him. The error must be caught before another pitch. If there had been no appeal prior to the pitch, the next batter would have been Charlie. Bill would have remained on first and sleepy Adam simply missed his turn.

HIT AND OUT

Q: A batter hits a ball deep to right field that is cleanly fielded after it hits the ground. The batter rounds first and heads for second without pausing. He is thrown out by the right fielder. Is the batter credited with the hit? —*Tony Righellis, Lorain, OH* [5/31/91]

A: Absolutely. He is credited with a single and is out trying to stretch it.

HITTING AN ILLEGAL PITCH

Q: The umpire called "illegal pitch." The batter, having no time to comply, hit the illegal pitch and grounded out. The umpire called batter out. Did the umpire make the right call? If so, please explain the ruling. —*Ben Catalano, Downington, PA* [4/10/98]

A: I presume you are asking about slow-pitch softball. In this case, if an umpire calls "illegal pitch" and the batter swings at the ball, the "illegal pitch" call is erased and whatever happens on the swing stands. If it's fast-pitch softball, the swing is erased only if the batter reaches first safely and all other runners advance at least one base. In that case, the play stands. Otherwise, in fast-pitch, all runners are advanced one base and it becomes a ball on the batter. In baseball, it would be a balk and the action would be the same as in fast-pitch baseball, except the batter isn't credited with a ball if he doesn't reach first safely.

THE GWRBI RULE

Q: Recently after a softball game we argued about who got the GWRBI (game winning run batted in). Our third batter knocked in the first run in the first inning. I knocked in the fourth run that made the score 4-0 in the first inning. One guy said I got the GWRBI because we won 17-3. I say our third batter got the game-winner because he hit the run that put us ahead to stay. Please give us the major league ruling. Is there a GWRBI in softball? —*John Summerville, Mentor* [8/1/85]

A: The GWRBI is the one that gives the team a lead it never relinquishes. This is the official major league definition. When your third batter knocked in the first run, your team went ahead and never gave up that lead. Hence, he gets the GWRBI—if you have such a statistic in your league. Softball has no provision for an official GWRBI and it's just as well. It's a rather silly stat.

BLANK SLATE

Q: Please help settle what has turned into an annual spring argument between myself and a teammate. In the first game of the season, a batter grounds out four times and finishes with a .000 batting average. Another batter walks four times. What is the correct way to list his batting average? I say he has none . . . not even .000. My teammate claims all players start the season with a .000 average so it should remain .000. The 11th spot in a 10-man batting order awaits the loser. —*Tom Martosko, Cleveland, OH* [5/8/77]

A: Mathematically you are right. The batter has no batting average before the season opens and since he walked four times he still has no batting average after the first game. But in the baseball books, blanks are occupied by zeroes so although technically incorrect, the batter's average is listed at .000 before his first plate appearance and *after* it, if he happens to walk or fails to get a hit.

Why don't you both bat tenth?

·················· **DOUBLE PLAY GOES DOWN** ··················

Q: It is the bottom of the ninth with the score tied, runners on first and third and one out. The batter hits a routine grounder to the second baseman who throws to the shortstop for the force, but they are unable to turn the double play and the winning run scores. However, the batter broke his bat on the swing and upon inspection of the bat, after time is out, the umpire discovers the bat was corked, that he used an illegal bat. He calls the batter out. Do they go into the 10th inning? —*Stephen M. Bales, Lakewood, OH* [9/26/82]

A: Yes, the double play the defense failed to make now becomes one. The runner is forced at second and the batter is out for cheating. Go into extra innings.

·················· **THAT BALL IS DEAD** ··················

Q: Here is the situation: Indians playing Seattle, August 15. Bobby Bonds was on first base and Andre Thornton hit a drive down the right field line. The ball hit inside the foul line and the right fielder *touched* it with his glove and then the ball bounced into the stands. The umpire ruled it was a double and Bonds, who had scored, was sent back to third base. And he never scored that inning. It does not seem right that Bonds could not score if the right fielder touched the ball. Bonds had rounded third before the ball was touched, according to Joe Tait. What's the rule? —*Earl Turner, Shaker Heights, OH* [9/9/79]

A: Unless the fielder purposely knocks the ball into the stands— which he didn't—this is a ground-rule double. The ball is dead, and all runners advance two bases from where they were at the time the pitcher took his position on the rubber. Therefore, the umps were correct in holding Bonds at third.

Out of Left Field

Q: Last winter while vacationing in Mexico, I had the pleasure of watching a baseball game in the Mexican League. I witnessed a very unusual play and would like your expert opinion on the umpire's ruling. The batter hit a sinking line drive into right field which got by the right fielder. Before he could run the ball down, a pig ran onto the field and swallowed the ball. The umpire immediately ruled that it was an "Inside the Pork" home run. How do you see this one? —*Mike Popelas, Willoughby, OH* [1/31/85]

A: Seriously, if an animal does run onto the field and grabs the ball, the umpire should give the batter as many bases as he thinks the batter would have made if there hadn't been this interference. I sense something's not kosher about this play.

WHAT GOES AROUND . . .

Q: Could you please explain the ruling on whether or not a batter "goes around" for a strike call? What do the first and third base umpires judge by when they are asked to make this call? —*Kenny Smith, Mansfield, OH* [9/10/87]

A: If any part of the bat crosses the plane of home plate, it's a strike. Of course, it's tough for an umpire at first or third to make that fine distinction, but it's part of the job. Before television almost every checked swing was called a ball. But TV replays revealed over and over again that the bat actually did go far enough. So now, most checked swings become strikes because umpires have been made aware that once a swing begins it's difficult to stop it before the bat reaches the plate. Thus, in a sense, there is instant replay in baseball and it has made a definite impact on the game.

NO RBI HERE

Q: Some of my teammates and I are in an argument over the ruling on a run batted in. Is the batter credited with an RBI when a runner on third steals home? How about if the runner scores on an error, a passed ball, or a wild pitch? How about if he scores when the batter grounds into a double play? I say no RBI on all of these. My teammates say it is an RBI. Who's right? —*Keith Zellner, Schofield, WI* [5/18/79]

A: You're right on all counts. None of the above is a run batted in, for the batter *did not* bat in the run. And when he hits into a double play, he doesn't deserve credit for one.

.... **Out of Left Field** ....

Q: A man with a three-foot beard walks up the plate, the pitcher throws the ball and hits the beard. Does the batter get his base? —*Frank Pfeiffer, North Olmsted, OH* [7/3/64]

A: Yes. Also, a close shave.

.... **BROKEN WRISTS** ....

Q: Perhaps I missed something you could correct me on concerning the "half swing." I thought that when the batter broke his wrists, this was a strike. Isn't this the test? Or am I missing something? —*Tom McCafferty* [5/18/79]

A: This is a common misconception. There is no such thing as the batter "breaking his wrists" in order to make a swing legal.

The rules book gives no definition for a swinging strike except to say a strike is a "pitch struck at by the batter." If the ump thinks the batter *struck* at the ball—that's it, a strike.

Once, during a World Series game, the Western Union ticker tape giving the play-by-play said, "DiMaggio broke his wrists on a third strike." The copy editor picked up that line and put this headline on the story: "DiMaggio Breaks Wrists."

.... **ANOTHER DEAD BALL** ....

Q: Would you please give me the correct ruling on the following play that occurred in our summer baseball league? We have runners on first and second, two outs. The batter squares to bunt, but the pitch hits his leg and bounces away. The runners advance to second and third. The home plate umpire awards the batter first base. However, after an appeal, the base umpire calls the pitch a strike, saying the batter actually attempted to bunt it. He calls the ball dead and sends the runners back to first and second. We played the game under protest because we felt that if the pitch was a strike the ball should be live and the base runners free to advance on their own. We were winning, 4-0, at the time but failed to score in the inning and went on to lose, 5-4. No one I've talked to seems to know the rule for certain. Please settle the confusion. —*Jeff Fondriest, Dover, OH* [6/11/88]

A: When the batter swings at a pitch that hits him, the ball is dead immediately. It's a strike on the batter and no runners can advance. The base ump called it correctly. You lost the game and you lose the protest. Sorry about that.

BOUNCE IN THE BOX

Q: In a recent game we played, the pitcher pitched the ball and it bounced in front of the plate. The batter hit it in fair territory. There was an argument as to whether or not he was out. What was he? —*Norman Bernstein, Cleveland Heights, OH* [5/9/60]

A: It's perfectly legal for a batter to hit a bouncing pitch. But he must be inside his batter's box when he connects. If he isn't, he's out. Where was your batter? Remember, part of the batter's box extends into fair territory.

HIT IT AND RUN

Q: What if the pitcher pitches a ball which hits the ground, bounces over the plate and the batter hits it over the fence? Is it a home run? —*Mike Fitzpatrick, Marion, OH* [6/20/81]

A: Absolutely. If it bounces up fat, hit it and run. If it doesn't, let it go, for the ump will call it a ball.

FAIR IS FAIR

Q: This is a hypothetical situation and I would like to know how it is scored. With a runner on third and only one out, the batter hits a long fly to left. The runner on third tags up and waits for the catch. But the left fielder drops the ball and the runner trots home easily. I feel that since the left fielder made an error, the batter should be charged with an at-bat and no RBI should be given. My friend feels that since the error means "ball should have been caught," the batter should get a sacrifice and an RBI. Who is right? —*Glenn Kuhn, Sauquoit, NY* [7/16/78]

A: You friend has a logical mind. He's right. It would be unfair *not* to give the batter a sacrifice and an RBI. You wouldn't want to be unfair, would you?

························ **HAND OR BAT?** ························

Q: Last summer in Little League, the umpire made a call I didn't agree with so I'm asking you who was right. The batter was hit on the hand by a pitched ball that never touched his bat. The umpire said it was a strike. I said the batter should be awarded first base. He said the hand is part of the bat. Who's right? —*Louis Welby, Lorain, OH* [11/27/87]

A: If the batter didn't swing, the umpire was wrong. The hand is not part of the bat unless the batter swings. The batter should have been sent to first base for being hit by the pitch. When the umpire isn't sure if the ball hit the hand or the bat he'll examine the batter's fingers. If he sees a bruise he'll send the batter to first.

························ **BRUSHED OFF** ························

Q: The pitcher throws a brush-off inside pitch at the batter. The batter steps out of the box so he doesn't get hit. The pitch hits his bat for a single. Is the batter out because he stepped out of the box, or does he get the single? —*William Talos, Cleveland, OH* [7/5/81]

A: If I'm umpiring he gets the single. The purpose of the rule is to prevent the batter from moving out of the box in order to gain some advantage.

In this case he *had* to get out of the box and to call him out for doing so would be ludicrous.

················ **MAJOR LEAGUE ARGUMENT** ················

Q: In our slow-pitch league, this play often comes up: There are no outs and a man on first. The batter lines a single to center field but steps on the plate while hitting the ball. We know the batter is out for stepping on the plate while hitting the ball.

Now, what about the runner on base? I say he can run at his own risk. Some agree. Others say he has to stay on first. It's become a major league argument. Please settle it. —*Jimmy Wright, Warren, OH* [6/20/90]

A: Whenever a ball is batted illegally the play is dead immediately. No runners can advance. The batter is out and the runner must remain on first base. End of argument—I hope.

.... **FAIR OR FOUL?** ....

Q: This happened to me in a recent blooper game. Standing deep in the box, I topped the ball and it hit the ground behind home plate and bounced into fair territory. I was thrown out. I agreed with the umpire as I always thought this is a fair ball. Right? —*W. M. Knitter, Westlake, OH* [8/13/59]

A: Right. Players—including major leaguers—and fans seem to show more ignorance about this rule than any other. Most folks assume that because a ball first lands in foul territory it is a foul. It makes no difference where the ball first lands. If it is first *touched* by a player in fair territory, it is a fair ball. Backspin on a ball occasionally causes it to bounce foul and then roll fair.

However, a ball often hits the batter while he is still in the batter's box, then it bounces fair. Since the major portion of the batter's box is in foul territory, the umpire generally assumes the ball was foul when it hit the batter so he rules it a foul ball. We say "assumes" because it is almost impossible for the umpire to locate the exact line of demarcation between foul and fair from his position behind both the catcher and the batter on such a play. In your case, I'm sure that the umpire was mighty grateful you agreed with him.

.... **SWITCH ON THE PITCH** ....

Q: What we would like to know is if there is any rule which prohibits a batter from switching from one batter's box to the other, no matter what the count is on him. A few people, like myself, say that a batter can't switch after he has two strikes. The more I think about it, the more I think I'm wrong. —*Sgt. Edward A. Miller, Phoenixville, PA* [8/16/69]

A: That's right. You *are* wrong. A batter can switch on every pitch, just so he does it before the pitcher gets into his pitching position.

······················ **ONLY WITH A SWING** ······················

Q: In a Little League tournament game, our batter was hit on the hand by a pitch. The umpire ruled that since his hand was on the bat, even though the ball hit the hand and not the bat, this was considered a foul ball and not a hit batsman. The batter was jumping out of the way and neither his bat nor his hand was in the strike zone and he was not attempting to swing. Was this the correct call? —*Jodie Andrews, Warren, OH* [6/28/90]

A: No. The hand is part of the bat only when the batter takes a swing. The batter was hit by a pitch. He should have been awarded first base.

······················ **IS THE STREAK OVER?** ······················

Q: I remember a game in the mid-1970s when Dave Kingman hit three consecutive homers for the Mets at Dodger Stadium. Kingman was walked in his next plate appearance. Did the walk break his consecutive homer string? Would an intentional walk be considered as breaking a consecutive homer string? Also, if a player is intentionally walked in all his plate appearances in a particular game would his consecutive game hitting streak be broken? —*Howard Hofmann, New Philadelphia, OH* [5/7/87]

A: Bases on balls, intentional or otherwise, never break a batting streak of any kind. It's not the batter's fault if the pitcher doesn't give him anything good to hit.

······················ **KEEP COUNT** ······················

Q: Please settle this big argument: Can a pinch hitter replace a batter after the batter has a count on him? For instance, if the batter has a 2-1 count and he isn't injured, can he be replaced by a pinch hitter? —*Hod Dean, New Philadelphia, OH* [7/11/85]

A: Yes, a batter can be replaced no matter what the count. The same count continues on the pitch hitter.

······················· **DROP THAT BAT** ·······················

Q: The other day I bunted down the third base line and they couldn't make a play on me. While running to first I had forgotten to drop my bat, so I dropped it after touching first. The umpire called me out. Was he right? —*Tom Talcott, North Olmsted, OH* [8/5/60]

A: Not if he's going by the official rules book. He's going by some myth that was started many years ago. It's legal to carry your bat to first, providing it doesn't interfere with the defense in any way. Actually it serves as a handicap to the runner, slowing him down.

The only time you should use a baton is in track. Or if you're an orchestra leader.

······················· **ANYONE CAN DH** ·······················

Q: In the American League today, with the designated hitter rule, even a good hitter does not bat in a game in which he is pitching. However, is there a rule against his batting, either as a pinch hitter or designated hitter, in a game in which he is not pitching? Or would this make a mockery of the rule? —*James Allison, Lorain, OH* [1/4/03]

A: It's perfectly legal for a pitcher to be used as a pinch hitter or designated hitter in a game in which he's not pitching. In fact, he could hit in a game in which he's pitching if the manager thinks he's better than any designated hitter he might use. The team simply would forfeit its DH rights for that game. Babe Ruth started out as a pitcher. If he were pitching today, no doubt he'd be hitting, too. Every day.

······················· **IT'S OFFICIAL** ·······················

Q: I play CYO baseball. In my first game, I was at bat three times. The first time up I was safe on an error and knocked in two runs. The second and third times I lined singles into left field. I thought that my batting average would end up 1.000 with four RBIs. I thought they would put the error as an unofficial time at bat. But it ended up as a .666 average. Why would an error be counted as an official time at bat and I did not even make an out? —*John Ciclecen, Wickliffe, OH* [5/17/80]

A: It is an official time at bat because you would have made an out if the fielder hadn't made an error. Your batting average was figured correctly.

······················· **OUTSIDE THE BOX** ·······················

Q: Batter attempts to bunt on the first pitch. In doing so he steps on home plate. If the ball is bunted fair, is he out? What if the ball is bunted foul? —*Bill Galchick, Salem, OH* [6/22/75]

A: The batter is out anytime he hits the ball—fair or foul—with at least one foot completely out of the box.

   On your play he'd have to be out unless he had awfully big shoes.

······················· **NEVER ASSUME** ·······················

Q: Here's a play up for discussion: There's one out in the top of the ninth, the Tigers are leading the Indians, 4-3, Jack Heidemann is on third and Eddie Leon on second and Tony Horton is at bat. He strikes out but the ball gets away from Bill Freehan, the Tigers' catcher, and goes to the backstop. Horton, thinking it's only the second strike, remains at the plate. Heidemann heads home and scores the tying run. Leon tries to score from second but Freehan's throw to the Tigers' pitcher nips him at the plate. The pitcher then turns and tags Horton who is still at the plate. The Indians, assuming the score is tied, take the field. The Tigers protest, saying, "The game is over." What do you say? —*Nicholas R. Grubic, Lorain, OH* [6/20/70]

A: Before we answer this one, dear readers, what do you think the answer is? We're betting 90 percent would miss it. It's a dandy.

   Here's the rule: The game is over and the Tigers win, 4-3. Heidemann's run, even though scored when there was only one out, doesn't count. It was wiped out when Horton was tagged before reaching first base, completing a double play.

   The rule: "A run is *not scored* if the runner advances to home base during a play in which the third out is made by the batter-runner before he reaches first base."

If this doesn't seem fair, remember that if Horton had dashed to first he'd have made it safely and the run would have counted. But let's not blame Tony. If this really happened he'd have known the correct count. Right, Tony?

SOFTBALL SNAFU

Q: This happened in a tournament slow-pitch softball game. The batter stands deep in the box, but is legally inside it when he hits the ball. The catcher crouches very close to the batter, almost under him. The umpire moves up, close to the catcher. The batter swings and hits a fly to the outfield, which is caught. But as he swings, his bat hits the umpire. What's the call? The umpire ruled it no pitch and had the batter remain in his box.
—(An ASA umpire, name and address withheld by request) [8/9/76]

A: Since this strange play isn't covered by the rules, my immediate guess was that the umpire could do whatever he thought proper and it would be legal. But just to make sure, I checked with Tom Mason, the national official softball interpreter. His reply: "The out stands. This is not umpire interference."
Let that be a lesson to you umpires. Don't crowd the catcher. If you want to get that close to the batter's box, join a team.

WHEN THE PITCHER MUST BAT

Q: A glass of sarsaparilla rides on this one: Top of the first, two outs. The visiting team has scored three runs and now has the bases loaded for the pitcher, who is batting ninth. This is a National League game so there is no DH. Can the visiting manager yank the pitcher for a pinch hitter? Or must the announced pitcher face at least one batter (as is the case with relievers?) *—Leopold Froenlich, Forbes Magazine, New York (former resident of Willoughby, OH)* [7/23/87]

A: The announced starting pitcher for each team must pitch to at least one batter and that batter must complete his turn at bat. Therefore, in your situation, a pinch hitter could not be used. The announced starting pitcher must bat for himself. Hope joining Forbes has proved to be a good investment for you.

··············· **A DIFFERENT KIND OF SACRIFICE** ··············

Q: It is late in the final game of the season. One out, and George
Brett needs another hit to bat .400. Willie Wilson is leading off
second and sees Brett's grounder will hit him if he stays where
he is. It does. Of course, Wilson is out. But does Brett get credit
for a hit? —*Rev. Raymond Howe, Tukhamonk, PA* [9/28/1980]

A: It the umpire doesn't call Wilson out for intentionally trying
to break up a double play, and I doubt if he would on the play
you describe, the scorer must give Brett a hit, according to the
present rule.

I think it's a bad rule because a pitcher could lose a no-hitter
on such a ground ball. And one of these years when it happens,
the rule will be changed and the batter no longer will be credited with a base hit when his batted ball hits a runner.

But the simple answer is, yes, Wilson's thoughtfulness would
give Brett .400. That's teamwork.

3

On the Paths

Questions about Base Running

·················· **RUNNING STARTS** ··················

Q: Can a base runner who is tagging up on a fly ball get a running start? For example: Can a runner on third base, upon a fly ball hit to the outfield, go back to the outfield grass along the third base line and start running toward home along the line, tag the base as the ball is caught and proceed towards home?
—*Dan Coleman* [7/2/72]

A: No, the rules specifically forbid this. Flying starts are illegal and upon appeal the runner would be out for failing to tag up properly.
Touch—and go.

·················· **NO FORCE WITH YOU** ··················

Q: This is the situation: There are runners on second and third with one out. The batter hits a long fly to center field, both runners advancing after the catch. However, on appeal, the runner from second is called out for leaving the base before the catch. Does the run count? —*Robert Bullington, Rocky River* [9/7/69]

A: The third out wasn't a force. Nor was it made by the batter before he reached first base. And the runner scored before the third out was made. *Therefore the run counts.*

···················· **A BALL IN THE HAND** ····················

Q: A player is caught in a rundown. The fielder tags the runner with his glove. He did not have the ball in his glove, but in his other hand. Is the runner safe or not? I called the runner out because I thought I read a similar question in your column in which you said the runner was out. Please tell me if my memory was right or wrong. —*Andre Parhamovich, Maple Heights, OH* [8/6/67]

A: Your memory was as wrong as the call. *A runner* must be tagged out with the ball or with the gloved hand while the ball is securely held in it.

My guess is that you read about a play in which the fielder held the ball in his bare hand but touched the *base* with his glove. That's legal. When tagging a base, the fielder can use any part of his anatomy, even his nose.

You see, there's a difference between a runner and a base.

···················· **JUDGMENT CALL** ····················

Q: Regarding the second game in the playoffs, between the Cleveland Indians and the New York Yankees: In the 12th inning, with Enrique Wilson on first, Travis Fryman bunted toward first base. Yankee first baseman Tino Martinez fielded the ball and threw to Chuck Knoblauch, who was covering first. Fryman was running inside the foul line and not in the three-foot lane just outside the line where runners are supposed to use on plays to first base. The ball hit Fryman on the back and rolled beyond first base. Knoblauch argued with the umpire who called Fryman safe and, by the time the ball was picked up by Knoblauch, Wilson scores and Fryman reached third. Why was Fryman called safe and what's the rule on this? —*Solon Kousman, Willard, OH* [10/17/98]

A: In the first place, the runner is *not* automatically out for failing to run in the ascribed path. He is out only if *in the umpire's judgment*, he was guilty of interference by not running in the lane. As I saw the play, after viewing it repeatedly from many angles, Fryman's foot reached the base just as the ball hit him. Since he was on the base—where he was supposed to be—he no longer was in a position to interfere with the throw.

Therefore, in my opinion, the umpire's call was right and the next day this was the consensus of all the umpires with whom I discussed the play. Had the ball hit him more than a yard from the base he would clearly have been out. But the Yankees, not expecting the bunt, fielded the ball too slowly. I do think the three-foot running path, which starts 45 feet from first base, should be shortened by at least a few feet. The runner on his last step must cut toward the base, since the base is in fair territory. But the path is in foul territory and if he remains in it all the way it's virtually impossible for him to touch first base. All umpires agree this is unfair to the runner and they allow him that last step inside the foul line. In any case, since Fryman already was at the bag, he was not out of the path.

······· **EJECTION REJECTION** ·······

Q: Suppose on that controversial play in the Indians-Yankees series (see above question) Knoblauch said some nasty words to the umpire while arguing with him and the ump immediately threw Knoblauch out of the game. In that case he couldn't have finally retrieved the ball and Fryman, as well as Wilson, might have scored. Would that have been possible?
—*Sal Trivisonno, Milford, CT* [10/19/98]

A: No. An ump can't eject a player while the ball is in play. And even if he inadvertently does, the ejection doesn't commence until after the ball is dead.

······· **NO SHORT CUTS** ·······

Q: Here is the situation that came up during an argument. There is a runner on first, one out. The hit-and-run is on, and the batter hits a long fly. The base runner makes it to third just as the outfielder catches it. I say the runner can cut across the diamond, by way of the pitcher's mound, to get back to first safely. But my manager, the umpire, the president of my Little League, my coach, my pitcher and even the benchwarmers say the base runner must tag second base on his way back to first. The reason I so staunchly stood my ground is that in your column a couple of years ago there was a similar argument in which the runner was safe by going back to first my way before

the throw. Please get this straight so I can win an easy $1.50.
—*Dale Tromski, Bedford, OH* [6/26/67]

A: Base runners must tag *all* bases in regular or reverse order.
You are wrong and you never read otherwise in this column.
Now the whole world is against you.

.... **BIG LEAGUE TIP** ....

Q: A line drive hits the runner standing on third base. Is the runner out? The ball then bounces high into foul territory and is caught by the third baseman before it hits the ground. Is the batter out? —*Tom Peabody* [6/16/60]

A: The runner was out the moment he was hit by the line drive, and the ball is then declared dead. A runner who is touched by a *fair* ball—while *on* or off the base—is *out* if the ball hasn't previously touched a fielder. The batter gets credit for a single and is given first base.

Here's a big league tip: A smart base runner, when on third, *always* takes his lead off in *foul* territory. If he's hit by a foul ball he's not out. The ball is dead immediately and *cannot* be caught.

.... **GIVING BACK A STEAL** ....

Q: Suppose a runner steals second base, but thinks the ball was fouled off and returns to first. Does he get credit for a stolen base? —*Willis Mather, West Haven, CT* [11/28/98]

A: He gets nothing. He gave back what he stole.

.... **AHEAD OF THE PITCH** ....

Q: In your illustrious career as an umpire did this play ever occur? Bases are loaded, two outs, the count is 3-2 on the batter and while the pitcher winds up, the runner from third heads home and slides in ahead of the pitch. The pitch then comes in and is called strike three. Would the run count? —*Barry Attenson, South Euclid, OH* [7/1/60]

A: The run does *not* count. Here's the rule: "No runs shall be scored on a play on which the third out is made by the batter before he reaches first base safely."

Yes, I've called this play more than once in my illustrious, thank you, career. And in return, I've been called a few things.

THAT BALL IS DEAD

Q: Indians have bases loaded, nobody out. Rick Manning at bat. He hits grounder down first base line in fair territory. Ball strikes the bag and rebounds into the air. Rick is running down the first base line. He grabs the ball out of the air and then scampers around the bases and crosses home plate. All three men score ahead of him. Rick, of course, is automatically out. But do the three runs count? —*Bruce Stratton, Cleveland, OH* [8/31/80]

A: The ball is dead because of Rick's interference and the runners must stay put. The bases are still loaded and there is now one out. In fact, if the ump thinks Rick prevented a double play by his actions he could rule two outs.

Rick wouldn't do anything this foolish, would he?

POP FLY

Q: With a runner on third and one out, the batter hits a fly ball to short left. The left fielder catches it, but it pops out of his glove and the runner on third heads for home. The shortstop was near the left fielder and he catches the ball before it hits the ground. Could the shortstop throw to third and appeal for the out? Or would the run score? —*Shane Jacoby, New Haven, CT* [9/26/98]

A: The run counts. Judging by my mail, this play seems to happen almost every night. Remember this: the runner does not have to wait for the catch. He is free to take off the moment the ball is touched.

SHARP AND DIRECT

Q: If a batter swings at a pitch and foul-tips it straight into the catcher's mitt, is a runner on base allowed to try to advance without going back to tag up before doing so? —*Louis Willey, Mansfield, OH* [7/27/87]

A: Yes. A foul tip is a ball that goes sharp and direct into the catcher's mitt and is held by the catcher. This is the same as a missed strike and runners are allowed to try to advance just as they would on a strike the batter missed completely. Of course, if the catcher drops the ball it becomes a foul strike, the ball is dead and the runners must go back to their bases.

·················· **IT COUNTS, IT COUNTS** ··················

Q: There are runners on first and third with one out. The batter hits a long drive to center. At the crack of the bat the runner on first goes to second and the runner on third goes home. The center fielder makes a great catch for the second out. He relays the ball to first base for the third out and the defensive team runs off the field. Now, does the run score? —*Chuck Connell, Mansfield, OH* [6/9/90]

A: If I had a dime for every time I've been asked this question, I could buy myself an expensive Father's Day gift, except I don't need anything. The run counts. It scored before the third out during a play in which the third out was *not* a force out. Therefore, it *must* count.

·················· **AUTOMATIC OUT** ··················

Q: Last month Tim McCarver of the Philadelphia Phillies hit a ball out of the park with the bases loaded. But he passed the runner who was on first. I understand he received credit for a single and all the runs scored. What would have happened if this same situation had occurred with two outs? How many runs would have scored? —*Mel Moses, Jr., Lyndhurst, OH* [8/15/76]

A: The instant McCarver passed the preceding runner he was out. Thus, if this made the third out the only runs that would count would be those that crossed the plate *before* McCarver passed the runner.

Of course, when there are two outs *all* the other runners would be off with the crack of the bat so the above play couldn't happen. Unless, of course, you have some sleepy runners.

························· **ONE RBI ONLY** ·························

Q: My brother hit a ball into the gap in right center. He was safe at third easily. The right fielder threw the ball away, though, and my brother was safe at home. There was a runner on second when my brother hit the ball. Does my brother get two RBIs? —*Curtis Ruoff, Hamilton, OH* [8/8/85]

A: No. He gets one. He scored on the throwing error, so he didn't knock himself in.

························· **TAG UP AND TRY** ·························

Q: I have a question regarding when a base runner can advance after a fly ball is caught. I've heard that a runner can advance as long as the ball is caught in *fair* territory. Can a runner advance if the ball is caught in foul territory, say near the foul pole? —*Mike Sullivan, Cleveland, OH* [7/25/85]

A: He can tag up and try to advance after *any* caught fly, fair or foul. That's why, with a runner on third, sometimes fielders purposely drop foul flies. That forces the runner to stay put.

························· **RUNNING WILD** ·························

Q: Suppose the Indians are playing the Yankees in the eighth inning. The Indians are at bat and trailing, 3-1. After one out, Toby Harrah gets an infield hit and Rick Manning draws a walk. Bobby Bonds grounds to Bucky Dent at short and Manning races to second just ahead of Dent's throw to Willie Randolph. In an effort to nip Bonds, Randolph makes a tremendous heave at first. A good throw would have had Bonds, but the throw goes wild and lands in the Indians' dugout. Harrah scores. But where would the umpires place Manning and Bonds in order to avoid a protested game? —*Pat Dailey, Burlington, IA* [3/31/79]

A: Since this is the second throw by an infielder, each runner gets *two* bases from where he was the instant the throw was made. Inasmuch as Manning already had reached second, he is awarded home plate. Bonds had not yet reached first so he goes to second.

The score is now tied. I hope the Indians win.

················· **Out of Left Field** ·····················

Q: During a recent baseball game with a runner on second, the batter gets a base hit and the runner goes to third. The ball coming into the pitcher gets by and rolls about five feet. The runner on third now tries to come home. The pitcher tries to tag the runner coming home and tags him on his hair which was about shoulder length and was blowing out. Is he out or safe? —*Jerry Mullally, Maple Heights, OH* [7/6/75]

A: He's out by a hair.

····················· **RETRACE YOUR STEPS** ····················

Q: I am a 10-year-old very interested in baseball and my uncle always asks me questions about baseball rules. This one has me puzzled. There is a runner on second with one out. Batter hits a long, high drive to center. The runner on second takes off immediately. As he is rounding third he misses the bag but continues on. Halfway home he sees that the center fielder has made a diving catch. The runner then cuts across the field and beats the throw back to second. Is he safe because he missed third or is he out for not retracing his steps? —*Joey Caroscio, South Euclid, OH* [7/18/77]

A: He can't be safe if he missed third. In retracing his steps he must tag third. That's part of the retracing process. Since he didn't and since there was an appeal he is *out*.

Is your uncle trying to learn the answers from you, or does he know them?

····················· **HORRIBLE CALL** ····················

Q: My baseball team was involved in a controversial call. It was the top of the seventh and we were losing, 8-6. With two outs and runners on second and third—I was on third—the batter gets a base hit to right field. I come running in from third to score. As I come in I see the bat on the third base line. I grab the bat to get it out of the way for the runner behind me. As I pick up the bat to tag the plate the catcher was blocking the plate so I stuck my foot in between his feet to tag the base. Then, *without* knocking him over, I get out of the way to guide in the second runner. He scores, beating the throw, to tie the game. The home plate umpire points to me and says I was out for interfering with the catcher. I blew up and was thrown out. I think I was safe because the ball hadn't been thrown yet and I think the catcher was interfering with me because there was no play on me. Please give me the proper ruling. —*Mark Iacafana, Newbury, OH* [7/29/79]

A: Of course, I have only your description to go on. But if the play occurred exactly as you describe it, the umpire made a horrible call. The catcher is *not* permitted to block the plate unless he has the ball in his possession or the throw is upon him.

Unless you did something you didn't tell me, I can't see how you interfered. The catcher was the one who was guilty of interference. From this long distance both runs appear to have scored legally.

Did the blowup make you feel any better?

·················· **DON'T MISS THIRD** ··················

Q: Two outs, man on first. Batter hits a home run and misses third base. It is appealed properly and the batter is called out. Does the run count from first, since the batter missed third base before the run crossed home plate? —*Myron Schnelli, New Bremen, OH* [7/25/76]

A: The run counts. The batter wasn't out *until* the appeal was made and by that time the run had scored. Batter gets credit for a double.

Third base is such a nice base. Don't miss it.

·················· **LEVELS OF INDIFFERENCE** ··················

Q: In a Cubs-Mets game I saw on TV, Ryne Sandberg was on third and Mark Grace on first. On the next pitch, Grace took off for second and Mets catcher Mackey Sasser did not attempt to throw to second. Grace was credited with a stolen base, but I think it should have been ruled "defensive indifference," and not a stolen base. However, both my parents insist there is no such thing as "defensive indifference." Who is right? —*Janet Gribnitz, Lorain, OH* [8/24/90]

A: Quote this rule to your parents: "No stolen base shall be scored when a runner advances solely because of the defensive team's indifference to his advance." The keyword, however, is "solely." If the pitcher takes his stretch and looks toward first and the runner is off as soon as the pitch is made, it isn't complete indifference. The pitcher is trying to hold him close. The fact that the catcher held the ball to prevent a possible double steal doesn't kill the stolen base by the runner from first. The scorer was right. And so were you—partially. You told your parents the truth.

TRIPLE PLAY?

Q: Here's the situation: Girls' slow-pitch softball. No outs, runners on first and second bases. The batter hits a line drive to the first baseman which is dropped. The runner on first jumps off the base but isn't tagged out. The runner on second stays there. The first baseman picks up the ball and tags first and then throws the ball to the pitcher. Meanwhile the runner who jumped off first goes back to first. The pitcher who now has the ball tags second and third bases, saying the two runners had to run. The umpires agreed and so it was a triple play. I say the runners are safe at first and second because the batter was forced out, leaving first base open. Who is right? —*Larry Mack, Cuyahoga Heights, OH* [6/13/76]

A: Everybody is wrong except you. Isn't that a great feeling? When the batter was put out the runners no longer had to advance. They were entitled to remain at their original stations without being put out. Had the first baseman tagged the runner and *then* the base, she would have had a double play. Or if she had thrown to third immediately, and then if the third baseman had thrown to second, it would have been a double play. And if the second baseman then had thrown to first before the batter got there, it would have been a triple play.

But since none of these things did take place, only the batter is out. The other runners stay put. And the umpires . . . well, let's be kind and say they have much to learn.

GIVE HIM A PUSH

Q: A runner is caught in a pickle between second and third. As he tries to get back to second the second baseman is in his path and he has to run around him in an effort to return. He is tagged out. There was no contact. Is he out? Or should the umpire call "obstruction" on the infielder? —*Name withheld* [7/2/75]

A: The base path belongs to the runner in any rundown. A fielder can block it only *if he has possession of the ball*. In this instance I'm assuming the second baseman didn't have the ball while he was standing in the runner's path. If so, "obstruction" should have been called and the runner should have been awarded third base inasmuch as he previously had legally touched second.

Contact is not necessary on an obstruction play but a smart runner will purposely run into the fielder just to make sure the umpire sees it. Just give the fielder a push if he's in your way. It's a free ticket to the next base.

ON TO SIBERIA

Q: It's the last of the ninth. There are two outs, the bases are loaded, and the score is tied. The batter walks. The runner from third simply goes to the dugout without touching the plate. Is the game over with the home team winning? —*Jed Burt, Canton, OH* [5/5/61]

A: No. The runner is out "for obviously abandoning his effort to touch the next base." Send the runner to Siberia and start the tenth inning.

IT COUNTS, IT COUNTS

Q: Slow-pitch softball game, runners on second and third base, one out. Batter hits a deep fly to right field. Ball is caught for second out. Both runners tag and advance. Shortstop asks for ball to make an appeal, says runner on second left too soon.

Proper appeal is made. Umpire calls runner out. Does the run count? —*Ray Anecki, Lorain, OH* [5/2/85]

A: This play comes up repeatedly every season. Every time it does, there's an argument. Perhaps this will help settle some of the dust. The run *counts*. It scored before the third out on a play that wasn't a force. The runner on second wasn't forced to go anywhere. It counts, counts, counts.

················· **HONEST, IT COUNTS!** ·················

Q: We have seen this situation twice recently with the umpires being undecided which way to call it. Would appreciate the final verdict from you. Men's slow-pitch softball: Runners on second and third, one man out. Fly ball hit to the outfield and caught for Out No. 2. Runner at third tags up and comes in to score. Runner on second fails to tag up and an appeal is made and he is called out for the final out of the inning. Does the run count, as it scored before the third out was made? —*Kenneth R. Miller, Wooster, OH* [6/2/76]

A: Yes, the run counts, since it did score before the third out was made. The only instances the run doesn't count if it scores before the third out is when that final out is on the batter before he reaches first base, or on a force play. The runner put out on the appeal at second didn't fall into either of these categories.

This is a simple play and I can't understand why so many players and/or umpires goof it up. I get at least three questions every week on this identical situation.

The run counts. It counts. Yes, it counts. Honest it does.

················· **FORCED** ·················

Q: Bases loaded, two men out. Pitcher winds up and the runner on third streaks for home. The pitcher disregards the runner and the pitched ball is two-thirds home when the runner slides across home plate; but, batter bunts the ball and is thrown out at first base for the third out. Does the run count? —*W. A., Painesville, OH* [6/26/65]

A: No. No run can score on a play during which the third out is made on the batter before he reaches first base. The play begins with the pitch so it is of no consequence that the runners reached home before the pitch got there.

At least the runner got practice sliding.

········· **FROM THE GUYS** ·········

Q: Please try to find time to answer two questions for me and my friends at work. We are constantly arguing about these plays:

Runners on first and third, two men out. Runner on first attempts to steal second and is caught in a rundown. Runner on third breaks for the plate and crosses it before the man in the rundown is tagged. Does the run score?

Runner on second base, two men out. Batter gets a hit, scoring man from second, but batter is caught in a rundown between first and second. Does the run count? —*The Guys, Euclid, OH* [7/13/69]

A: In neither case was the third out a force play or on the batter before he reached first base. So count the runs and go back to work.

········· **THROW HOME** ·········

Q: What's the rule on this play which happened in our recent game. Two outs, runners on first and third. On the next pitch the runner on first attempts to go to second and is caught in a rundown. The runner on third scores before his teammate is tagged during the rundown. Does the run count or would this rule apply: "Any runner is out after he has acquired possession of a base, if he runs the bases in reverse order for the purpose of confusing the defense or making a travesty of the game. The umpire shall immediately call time and declare the runner out." —*Tim and Mark Iacofano, Lyndhurst, OH* [7/2/77]

A: The run definitely counts. This was not a case of running the bases in reverse order for the runner never got to second. Had he made second and then tried to scoot back to first in an obvious effort to get caught in a rundown, so the man on third would try to score, you would have a legitimate argument. But in your situation you have a legitimate play instead.

The defense was outsmarted. Next time throw home.

.... **SLIDING INTO FIRST** ....

Q: Are you allowed to slide into first base? —*Jeff Janosek, Sheffield Lake, OH* [7/2/72]

A: Yes, but it's foolish to do unless you are trying to avoid a tag. Running gets you there faster than sliding and it saves on your mom's laundry bill.

.... **DEAD BALL WALK** ....

Q: We had a very interesting thing come up in one of our ASA slow-pitch softball games. With a runner on first base, two outs, the next batter walks. The runner on first overruns second and the catcher throws the ball to the shortstop who tags the runner while he is off the base. The umpire at home plate calls the runner out. But after a brief discussion with our manager the umpire reverses his decision, saying it was a dead ball when the batter walked. If the opposing manager wanted to protest the changed call when should the protest be filed? Also, what is the correct ruling on the runner who was tagged out? — *Earl DiFranco, Hamden, CT* [3/6/98]

A: In slow-pitch the ball is dead after a ball or strike. Therefore, the ball became dead when the batter walked, so the runner couldn't be tagged out after rounding second. But the instant the ball is returned to the pitcher the runner must go back to second. If he doesn't he's out. The ump was correct in reversing his decision. Protests must be declared before the next pitch. But in this case it would be a waste of time since there was nothing to protest.

.... **MISSING HOME** ....

Q: The bases are loaded. No outs. The batter hits a home run and as the runners go around the bases the man on first misses home plate. The batter who hit the home run touches all the bases and all the base runners return to the dugout. The catcher appeals the man who missed home plate and the umpire calls him out. Is this possible? If so, how many runs scored? What if there were two outs in the same situation? —*Charles Puell, Farrell, PA* [6/29/75]

A: In the first case, all the runners, except the one who missed the plate, have legally scored. Three runs count. In the second case, only two runs count because the runner from first made the third out when he missed home plate.

Of course, if that catcher hadn't been so alert, it would have been a grand slam in both cases.

NO ADVANCE

Q: Runners on first and second, one out. Batted ball hits runner going to second. I know the runner is out and the ball becomes dead. The question is this: I have always been told that a runner cannot advance on a dead ball, but in this case the runner on second was forced to break for third on the ground ball. Shouldn't he be entitled to third? What if he had been breaking for third with the pitch and already had reached there before the other runner was hit? Does he still have to go back to second? —*Ben Guesman, Niles, OH* [7/13/75]

A: No runners can advance on a play in which a runner is out because he was hit by a batted ball, unless the runner is forced to advance by virtue of the fact that the batter is awarded first base.

The play starts with the pitch, not with the hit. Get that runner back to second. He can't go a step farther. You now have runners on first and second, two outs.

MAKE IT A DOUBLE

Q: A runner is on first. Next batter hits a long drive. Runner is out at home while batter reaches third safely. Batter does not get a triple. Right or wrong? —*Arpad J. Gordos, Cleveland Heights, OH* [2/25/76]

A: Right. Batter receives credit for a double. He can't get three bases if the runner in front of him couldn't advance three bases, even if the runner was a truck.

A FOOT IN FOUL

Q: Here is a play that occurred in a Brook Park pitch tournament which caused quite a controversy. I think the umpires were reading something into the rules that just isn't there. Runner on first base with one foot on the base and the other in foul territory. Batter hits the ball over the fence but the umps rule the runner on first base out for "taking a sprinter's stance." The umps further said a runner is not allowed to stand with one foot in foul territory. I understand the umpires also were calling runners out for the same thing on second and third base. Runners have been doing this for years and have never been called out before. Were they right? —*Several Irate Managers* [7/2/78]

A: The umpires were wrong. They have dreamt up a rule that doesn't exist. On a fly ball it would be illegal to get a running start with *both* feet *behind* the bag but it is perfectly legal for a runner to position himself with one foot behind the base and one foot on it any time. It's also legal to keep one foot in foul territory.

THE THREE-FOOT RULE

Q: Argument, slow-pitch softball: Other fellow claims batter-base-runner must keep to the outside of the baseline to first base, within the three-foot limit. I claim he may run to first within the three–foot limit. I claim he may run to first within three feet of either side of the baseline. —*Joe Dober, Brecksville, OH* [9/12/76]

A: That three-foot line, of course, only pertains to the last 30 feet to first base. The runner doesn't have to stay within that space unless there is a play on him with which he might interfere. In other words, he's *not* automatically out if he doesn't run in that area. He's out only when he runs outside the three-foot line *and* in the opinion of the umpire he interferes with a fielder taking a throw at first base.

If no play is being made on him he can deviate even more than three feet from either side of the line.

Now you figure out who won your argument.

THE RULE IS CLEAR

Q: In a Sunday Morning League slow-pitch game, there were runners on first and second, two outs when the batter hit an inside-the-park homer. The runner who had been on first missed third and, after the batter scored, an appeal was made at third. The ump agreed that the runner who had been on first missed the bag and he was called out. But the ump said the other two runs counted. Was he right? —*Andy Gruber, Willowick, OH* [8/24/76]

A: No. Only one run counts on this play. The rule is clear: "No succeeding runner shall score a run when the preceding runner has been declared the third out of an inning."

   Give the batter a double, take away the run. That's what the arbitration board would do if you protested. Did you?

···················· **THAT BALL IS DEAD** ····················

Q: There is a runner on first. The ball is hit between first and second. The runner going from first is hit by the ball. The second baseman picks it up and throws to first before the batter gets there. The umpire calls this a double play. I think that's wrong. What do you say? —*Duane Mellen, New Philadelphia, OH* [7/28/90]

A: I say you're right. The ump blew it. The instant the runner was hit by the batted ball he was out. The ball is dead, the batter is awarded first base and is credited with a base hit. Only if the runner purposely allowed the ball to hit him in an effort to prevent a double play would both the batter and the runner be out.

···················· **GOTTA TAG UP** ····················

Q: This happened in our women's softball league: Runner on first, no outs. The batter hits a hard line drive that is caught by the shortstop. With the runner about six steps off first base, the shortstop fires the ball to first but badly overthrows and it goes over the first baseman's head and out of play. The runner had started back to the bag, but when she saw the overthrow, took off and was awarded third base by the umpire. Was it necessary for her to tag up at first before advancing, or is she no longer obligated to do so because of the overthrow? —*Carol Codney, Willoughby, OH* [8/29/85]

A: She must retouch first base before advancing. If she doesn't, she would be out on an appeal when the ball is put back into play. Even though the ball is dead, she had to retouch first before touching second. Once she touches second, she no longer can return to first and she's a sure out if the defense appeals that she left first too soon.

THEFT NOT ON RECORD

Q: With runners on first and third base, the runner on first breaks for second. He draws no throw and is credited with a stolen base. In the 1930s it was merely said the runner took second base unmolested. Has there been a change in the rule, or did the runner get a stolen base then? —*Peter Longo, Cleveland, OH* [6/7/66]

A: The runner didn't get one then and he doesn't get one now if, in the official scorer's judgment, the defensive team was indifferent to his advance.

If the defense pays no attention to a runner who is trying to steal he is committing the theft without it going on his record.

LEGAL LEFT TURN

Q: Batter beats out an infield hit and when returning to first he turns left instead of right. I say this is perfectly legal providing the runner makes no effort to advance to second. I've seen this play 100 times in your column, but I would appreciate a quick reply to clarify it. —*Bill Dillon, Lorain, OH* [6/19/77]

A: For the 101st time, it's legal to turn either way after passing first base, provided the runner makes no break for second. I'll probably be asked to run this answer 99 more times. It appears to need constant clarification. Maybe the signs should be posted at first base, "left turn permitted."

NO-COUNT STEAL

Q: Suppose there are two outs with a runner on third. The pitcher is taking his full windup so the man on third tries to steal home. There are two strikes on the batter at the time of the pitch and the pitch is strike three. However, the speedster from third slides home without being tagged and *before* the pitch has crossed the plate. Does the run count? —*Charles Carey, Mayfield Heights, OH* [3/6/98]

A: No. The fact that the runner reached home before the pitch is of no consequence. He can't score on a pitch which retired the batter for the third out.

·················· **KNOW YOUR OUTS** ··················

Q: This happened in a Senior Little League game which was protested and we would like the proper ruling. One out, runner on third, the batter pops out to the second basemen. The team on the field, thinking it was the third out, leaves the field. The runner on third also leaves his base and goes into the dugout to get his glove. The catcher, before going into the dugout, thinks maybe there are two outs, returns to the field, picks up the ball by the pitcher's mound and appeals to the umpire that the runner is out for leaving his base, making the third out. The third base umpire calls the runner out. The manager now protests that the runner should be allowed to return to third base and the game continued with two outs, claiming the fielding team confused his runner by leaving the field and even more, that the three umpires didn't know there were only two outs. —*Joe Ferra, N. Madison, OH* [8/29/82]

A: It is the responsibility of the runner to know how many outs there are. If he had walked home the run would have counted. When he went to the dugout to get his glove he was automatically out for abandoning his base. No appeal was needed. The defense gave him a break and he failed to take advantage of it. Incidentally, coaches are supposed to remind runners how many outs there are. This coach apparently was sleeping, too.

Simply put, inasmuch as the umpires didn't call time the runner *must* be called out.

·················· **TAG AND GO** ··················

Q: In a girls' fast-pitch softball game, no outs, runners on first and second, the batter hits a high fly to the first baseman. Umpire calls "infield fly, batter is out." The girl on second was off the bag and went to third base, but did not tag up before going there. Does she have to tag up? I said yes. They said no. Who's right? —*Martin Vosch, Hubbard, OH* [7/1/88]

A: You are. Except for the fact that the batter is automatically out, an infield fly is the same as any other fly with respect to the rules. Runners can try to advance at their own risk. But they must tag up before doing so—if the ball is caught.

············· **READY FOR TAKE-OFF** ·············

Q: Slow-pitch softball game. No outs, runner on first. Batter hits a line drive to the pitcher. The ball bounces out of his glove. Runner sees the ball bounce out and then takes off for second. The second baseman runs in and catches the ball before it hits the ground. He then throws to first and the runner is called out as he was sliding back to the bag. He was not tagged. I contended to the umpire that the runner legally could take off as soon as the ball hit the pitcher's glove and that he must be tagged to be put out, not the bag. He disagreed. Who was right? —*Carmen N. Ricco, Willoughby Hills, OH* [11/16/89]

A: You're right. The runner can leave his base the instant the ball is touched. He doesn't have to wait until it finally is caught. On your play, since the runner didn't leave too soon, there was no opportunity for an appeal. Therefore, the runner would have to be tagged while off base in order to be put out.

············· **LAZY OUT** ·············

Q: In baseball, a batter runs to first base. He gets there safely but overruns the base and stands beyond first base, making no attempt to return to the bag. He is then tagged. Is he safe or out? —*Karl Newyear, Willoughby, OH* [2/16/84]

A: The rule requires the runner to return to first base promptly. If he is too lazy to do so he deserves to be tagged out.

············· **ON HIS OWN** ·············

Q: As statistician for my son's Hot Stove team, I have a scoring problem. When a runner steals home who gets the RBI? —*Margie Johns, North Olmsted, OH* [6/27/80]

A: Nobody. RBI means run batted in. Nobody batted in the stealer. The thief did it on his own.

················· **DOUBLE PLAY DEBATE** ·····················

Q: Man on first base, no outs. Batter hits grounder to first base-man. Runner doesn't leave first base. First baseman tags him while he is standing on the bag, then steps on first. After quite an argument umpire calls it a double play. After discussing this play for two weeks with about 100 people we're still not sure. There are at least 20, including me, who say the umpire was wrong. Would you please give the correct ruling? —*Vic Nathal, Erie, PA* [6/28/70]

A: The umpire and the majority are right. It's a double play. The instant the ball is hit the runner no longer has a right to occupy first base. It belongs to the batter. So when the runner is tagged, he's out. Then when the bag is touched the batter is out. This is the correct way to make the double play.

   If the first baseman had tagged the base first the batter would be out and first base no longer would belong to him. Then the runner could stand there without jeopardy.

   Now I have a question: Why did it take an argument to convince the umpire? And if the argument was so good why didn't it convince you?

················· **DOUBLE PLAY OR NOT?** ·····················

Q: Bases loaded, one out. Batter hits a grounder to the third base-man, who fields the ball and starts for third base, then sees the runner on third has not started for home but is still standing on third. The third baseman tags the runner standing on third and then steps on third, forcing the runner from second. I contend this is a double play, since the runner on third had lost his right to the base once the batter hit the ball. The other side contends the runner couldn't be tagged out while standing on the base. What is the proper ruling? —*Dale Buclauer, Elkins, AK* [6/7/80]

A: It's a double play. The fielder handled it perfectly. The instant the ball was hit, first base belonged to the batter. Therefore, everybody else was forced to move on. Since third base no longer belonged to the runner who was there, he was out when tagged.

If the fielder initially had tagged the runner going to third, the force would have been off and the runner on third could have remained there. But since it wasn't made that way, the man on third's new home was home and he didn't go there. Therefore, he's out.

BEG YOUR PARDON

Q: Last Friday I was playing shortstop. A friend of mine, on the other team, was on second. A pop fly was hit to me and just as I was about to catch it he runs into me. I say he is out and he says he's entitled to hit me when I'm on the baseline. Who's right? —*Chris Thomas, Lakewood, OH* [5/16/63]

A: You are. The runner *must* avoid the fielder attempting to field a batted ball. I hope your friend at least said, "Pardon me."

GUILTY OF OBSTRUCTION

Q: Can the catcher block home plate if a runner is coming from third and the ball is being thrown home? Or must he have the ball in his possession in order to legally block the plate? —*Bill Galchick, Salem, OH* [6/25/75]

A: Anytime a fielder blocks the base paths without the ball he is guilty of obstruction. In the case you describe, if the umpire calls it—and he should—the runner would be awarded the plate.

The base paths are not supposed to be an obstacle course.

NEW WAY TO LOSE

Q: The Yankees are playing the Indians and Cleveland has a runner, Brett Butler, on third with one out. Joe Carter lifts a foul pop down the left field line. Mike Pagliarulo chases it down and made the catch, spins, and fires as Butler tags up and attempts to score. Pagliarulo's throw, however, hits the Indians' third base coach, Johnny Goryl, squarely in the back. Do the umpires allow Butler to score? Send him back? Call him out? Something else? —*Guy Henrich, Lorain, OH* [4/30/87]

A: The coach must make a legitimate effort to get out of the way of the throw. Since it hit him in the back, he obviously wasn't even watching the ball. So, if the throw had any chance to get Butler the umpire would call interference on Goryl and call Butler out. You figured out a new way for the Indians to lose a run.

·················· **PLEASE DON'T SQUEEZE** ··················

Q: Say the Indians are playing Oakland. It's the bottom of the ninth with the Tribe trailing, 10-9. Mel Hall is on third base with two outs and Brook Jacoby is at bat. He executes the suicide squeeze. The pitcher fields the ball and throws Jacoby out long after Hall crosses the plate. Does the run count?
—Aaron Simmons, Lorain, OH [7/7/88]

A: No. That's why the squeeze is never attempted with two outs. No run can score on a play in which the third out is made by the batter before he reaches first base.

·················· **SAFE IN THE DUGOUT** ··················

Q: Situation: Score tied, bottom of the last inning and home team puts men on second and third, with nobody out. Batter flies to left. Fielder makes the catch (one out) and throws to the plate trying to get the runner on third, who has tagged up and is going to the plate. Play is close but the runner scores.

Game appears to be over with winning run scoring, and plate umpire starts walking toward home team dugout. Defensive team does not leave the field, but appeals that runner on third left for plate before catch was made. Field umpire calls runner (who had scored winning run) out. The runner who had been on second had tagged third and touched home plate on his way to the dugout, following runner who had been on third. Although he was in the dugout after the successful appeal for the second out, the umpire ruled he (runner from second) was now the winning run.

Question: Is he the winning run? Why? Shouldn't he have been returned to third? Why? *—Martin E. Davis, Overland Park, KS* [9/19/76]

A: The umpire was right. The runner from second now becomes the winning run. The ball never was declared dead. If it had been dead, there could have been no appeal at third during a dead ball situation.

Since the ball was in play, and since there were fewer than three outs, the run must count. A following runner never is affected by the actions of a runner ahead of him unless that runner becomes the third out.

Give the runner on second credit for heads-up baseball. Or maybe he was just running for exercise. Either way, it paid off.

.... **BASEPATH MINUET** ....

Q: Indians vs. Royals: Mel Hall is on first. Joe Carter hits one in the gap in left center. Hall, that sterling base runner, gets charging around third but stops part of the way home and returns to third just as Carter and the ball arrive there. Both runners are now on third. As George Brett tags Carter, Hall momentarily steps off third. As Brett then goes to tag Hall, he steps on third and Carter steps off. How long can this "dance" go on? —*Ken MacDonald, Westlake, OH* [12/3/87]

A: The base belongs to Hall. Thus the dance can continue until Carter is tagged while on the base or either one of them is tagged while off it. I'd pay a lot to see this minuet.

4

On the Mound

Questions about Pitching

················· **JACK'S A JOKER** ·················

Q: Please settle a debate that arose after a recent softball game. Top of the first inning. Visiting team leads off with a single. Then the second baseman drops a pop fly for an error. The next batter singles to load the bases with no outs. The next two men pop up, the runners holding. The visitors now proceed to score 12 runs before the third out is made. I claim that *all* 12 runs are unearned. One-eyed Jack, my stubborn manager, disagrees. Please straighten him out. By the way, we came back and won, 15-13. —*Tom Guzowski, Brook Park, OH* [7/20/78]

A: For the second baseman's sake, I'm so glad. All the runs are *unearned*. One-eyed Jack must be a joker.

················· **WRONG PITCHER** ·················

Q: Suppose that one pitcher started a game by serving several hits and a few bases on balls to the opponents and is yanked without retiring a man. A relief pitcher is brought in and pitches hitless ball for nine full innings. Would the records show that he pitched a no-hit game? —*Steve Saferin, Beachwood, OH* [3/10/60]

A: We wrote to the publisher of the "Little Red Book" which contains all such records. His reply: "It is the game that counts. In this case it was not a no-hit game, but nine innings of hitless ball by a relief pitcher and would be so designated.

It also should be noted that in your example, the manager started the wrong pitcher.

· · · · · · · · · · · · · · · · · · · **ALONG CAME JONES** ·

Q: The Indians are playing the Yankees at the Stadium, no score, top of the ninth. There are two outs and Mel Hall triples off starter John Farrell. Doug Jones replaces Farrell and, without throwing a pitch, picks Hall off third base. The Indians score in the bottom of the ninth and win, 1-0. Who gets the win, Farrell or Jones, who never made a pitch? —*Michael Kennedy, Painesville, OH* [7/27/89]

A: Jones is the winner because he was the pitcher of record when the winning run was scored. I can picture George Steinbrenner screaming at Hall after this one.

· **TRICKY MOVE** ·

Q: Runners on first and third. Pitcher comes to a set position, right foot in contact with the rubber. He steps directly toward third, fakes throw. Then, with right foot as pivot foot and still in contact with rubber, whirls and throws to first. No balk? —*Richard Wiley, Bedford Heights, OH* [4/28/75]

A: No. It's a tricky move but a good one and has been tried in the majors several times. Just don't get your feet tangled.

· **NOT PERFECT** ·

Q: A perfect game is one where the pitcher gives up no runs, hits and walks, and his teammates make no errors. Would it be considered a perfect game if the pitcher struck out the batter and, due to either a wild pitch or a passed ball, the batter was able to reach first? —*Charles Smithson, Mansfield, OH* [10/19/84]

A: You have the wrong definition of a perfect game. It's one in which no player from one team reaches first base. Thus, in your example, the no-hitter would not be a perfect game. Incidentally, it's possible for a pitcher to have a perfect game and yet have his team commit an error. Let's see, dear reader, if you can figure out how? We'll supply the answer next week.

PUZZLE ANSWER: Last week we asked, "How is it possible

to have an error committed in a perfect game?" Suppose a batter hits a foul ball and the catcher drops it. The catcher is charged with an error. The batter then makes an out and no batter reaches first base throughout the game. Thus, by definition, it's a perfect game. Actually you could have dozens of errors—dropped fouls—and the game still could be "perfect." I'll bet you were expecting a trickier solution.

THE REAL THING

Q: No outs, bottom of the ninth. Score is tied, 4-4. First batter in the inning singles. A relief pitcher is brought in. Next batter hits into a forced out at second. Now there are two outs and a different runner on first. The next batter triples to win the game. Which pitcher receives the loss in this situation? —*Greg Mandler, Peoria, IL* [6/28/77]

A: The pitcher who started the inning gets the loss. He put the winning run on base. The force merely substituted a runner for the man he put on. In this case substitutions don't count. Only the real thing.

Out of Left Field

Q: It's not baseball season but here's a play that happened this summer we're still talking about. The first batter in the inning hits a line drive to the fence. The runner tags first base, continues to second base—but misses the bag—and then goes to third base. The throw from the outfield to third is late and the third base umpire calls the runner safe. The ball is then thrown to the pitcher. The defensive team manager asks for time and goes to the mound. He puts his arm on the pitcher's shoulder and calls his infielders to the mound for a huddle. He tells his pitcher to get on the rubber and then throw the ball to the shortstop, who should then appeal to the second base umpire that the runner did not touch second base.

The manager leaves the mound, the pitcher gets on the rubber, raises his pitching arm, and throws to *third* base. As he throws to third base, the third base umpire calls a balk. The third base ump sends the runner home.

Now the manager comes back to the mound, repeats the

same instructions and leaves. The pitcher gets on the mound and this time he throws the ball to the shortstop who makes the appeal at second. The ump says he can't accept the appeal because the ball is dead, since time had been called by the plate umpire and he had not called "play ball." So the pitcher gets the ball again, returns to the rubber and the umpire says, "Play ball." The pitcher then steps off the rubber, throws to second for the appeal and the umpire there calls the batter out for failing to touch second. Was this correction? You don't have to hurry with your answer. I want you to give it some thinking.
—*Andrew Tablack, Campbell, OH* [2/21/74]

A: The answer is quite simple. The run counts. An appeal must be made *before* the next play. A balk is considered a play. Hence the balk wiped out the opportunities to appeal.

Hope you're not disappointed that the answer came so quickly. I didn't even have to look it up.

BLAME GAME

Q: Although I know that a run scored on a wild pitch is an earned run and is counted against the pitcher's earned run average, how would you score this one: With one out in the inning, the batter swung at a pitch in the dirt, striking out, but reached based when the catcher could not handle the wild pitch. A walk, single and hit batsman followed scoring the man who originally struck out. Is it an earned run? —*Harry Aukerman* [7/31/77]

A: Absolutely. The runner was put on base by the pitcher and he moved him around. Therefore, he gets full credit—actually blame—for the run.

ON THE SET

Q: With a runner on first, the pitcher starts his normal stretch. His hands have reached a face-high position and he has not yet come down to the set position. While coming down toward his belt, the pitcher throws to first base. His hands, at the time, are halfway between his face and his belt. Is that a balk?
—*Andy Dravecky, Eastlake, OH* [9/4/77]

A: Not if he steps directly toward first. It is necessary to come to the set position before throwing to the batter, but it's okay to throw to a base before the "set" is reached.

I hope this answer sets well with you.

.... **TAKE FIVE** ....

Q: A major league pitcher leaves the game after three innings with a 6-0 lead. The first reliever pitches the fourth inning and leaves, leading, 9-1. The third pitcher enters the game in the fifth inning. He finishes. The final score is 14-5. Who is credited with the win? —*John Hodgins, Lorain, OH* [5/3/91]

A: The starting pitcher *must* go five innings in order to be credited with a victory. So scratch him. The official scorer now must decide which of the two relievers pitched most effectively. He must make the judgment call. Most likely he'll give it to the final pitcher since he pitched the most innings.

.... ▐ **Out of Left Field** ▌ ....

Q: Lots of bets are on this one: Can a pitcher be the winner and loser in the same game? For example: Indians vs. Red Sox in a game played in April. Greg Swindell is pitching for the Indians. The game is suspended after the seventh inning with the score tied at 1. The game is completed in August. In the meantime, Swindell is traded to the Red Sox. He comes back and finishes the game for the Red Sox and they win, 2-1. Any way Swindell can be both the winner and loser? —*Bob Allen, Rob Schmidt, Ron Potesta, Warren, OH* [7/5/90]

A: In your scenario, Swindell would be the winner only. But if it happened this way he'd be both winner and loser: He retires the Red Sox to complete the seventh, score 1-1, and the game is suspended because the lights fail. It's continued in August and now Swindell has been traded and is pitching for the Red Sox. Top of the eighth. The Indians treat their old pal unkindly and immediately score a run. The Indians hang on to win, 2-1. But Swindell still was the Indians' pitcher of record when they scored the run that put them ahead to stay. Their new pitcher didn't become official until he went to the mound in the bottom half of the eighth. So Swindell has to be the winning pitcher, even though he gave up the run that cost the Red Sox the game. He also is the loser because he was the Red Sox pitcher of record, too, when the Indians scored the run that beat Swindell's new team. In other words, he was the pitcher of record for both teams at the same time and during that period the winning and losing run was scored.

SCORE V. ROCKY

Q: What uniform number did Herb Score wear when he pitched for the Indians from 1955-59? Also, what were the statistics when Rocky Colavito faced Herb from 1960-62? —*Tim Fillinger, Euclid, OH* [8/19/89]

A: Score wore No. 27. I asked him about his success, or lack of it, against his old roomie, Colavito. He recalls facing him about four times. "I can remember only one hit," says Score, "I had him 2-2 and then threw him a good curve. The ump called it a ball. I said to Rock, 'How could you take that one?' He just grinned. On the next pitch he topped a slow roller down third. It stayed fair and he was safe. I said, 'Now come on Rocky, you're not going to take that hit, are you?' He said, 'You bet.' We still laugh about that."

EARNED OR UNEARNED?

Q: Can a home run ever be an unearned run? —*Joan Ludwin, Parma, OH* [7/8/79]

A: If you just read the question and immediately said, "No," you're wrong. An unearned run is one the pitcher shouldn't be charged for. Suppose there are two outs. The next batter grounds to the shortstop who fumbles the ball for an error, permitting the batter to reach first safely. If the fielder hadn't fumbled there now would be three outs. So, any runs scored against the pitcher in this inning shouldn't have occurred. Thus, all of them would be unearned, even if the next batter comes up and hits a home run.

And even if the batter hit one into the stadium bleachers, an unprecedented feat, it would be an unearned run under the above circumstances.

·················· HIDDEN BALL TRICK ··················

Q: With the runner on first, the first baseman huddles with the pitcher and hides the ball in his glove, hoping to catch the runner with the hidden ball trick. Time never was called. In order to lure the runner off the bag the pitcher toes the rubber, as if to pitch. The play works as the first baseman tags the runner when he starts taking his leadoff. Is this legal? —*Larry Milder, Lorain, OH* [10/6/90]

A: No, no, a thousand times no. The instant the pitcher steps on the rubber without the ball it is a balk. Send the runner to second base.

·················· EARNED RESPONSIBILITY ··················

Q: With two outs the third batter of an inning hits a triple. If the runner scores via a balk, wild pitch, or passed ball, isn't the run earned? Two sportscasters say the run is unearned. The next batter makes an out. —*Lloyd Leonard, Lorain, OH* [5/5/88]

A: An earned run is one for which the pitcher is responsible. He committed the balk, so that would be an earned run. He threw the wild pitch, so that would also be an earned run. The passed ball was the catcher's fault, not the pitcher's. So that run would be unearned. You won't find Herb Score making this mistake. As a pitcher he knew when he was responsible for a run. Besides, he has carefully read the rules book many times. More baseball announcers should.

·················· FOUR STRIKEOUTS IN ONE! ··················

Q: I have seen the records for pitchers who have struck out four batters in an inning. Seventeen pitchers have done it. I was wondering how a pitcher can strike out four batters if three outs make up an inning? —*Matt Morrill, Willoughby, OH* [8/24/88]

A: Suppose the first two batters strike out. The next batter strikes out on a pitch that is high and outside and goes past the catcher. The batter reaches first safely. That's still a strikeout even though the batter is now on first. The next batter also strikes out and this time the catcher holds onto the ball ending the inning on the fourth strikeout. Using the same scenario the strikeouts could go on indefinitely if the third strike continually goes past the catcher and the batter reaches first safely. As a matter of fact, the minor league record for the most strikeouts by one pitcher in one inning is six. Can you picture his frustration?

······························ **NO SAVE** ······························

Q: This is in regard to an Indians-Orioles game last month. When the game ended, the television announcers said Mike Jackson had just earned his 32nd save. But in the *USA-Today Baseball Weekly* publication, Steve Reed and Paul Assenmacher were credited with "holds" and Jackson got no save. Jackson's next save was credited to him two days later and was listed as No. 32. I thought it should have been 33. Why didn't Jackson get one for that game against the Orioles? —*Warren Terrell, Painesville, OH* [9/26/98]

A: The TV announcers were wrong. The Indians were leading, 6-3, going into the ninth. Assenmacher started the ninth and retired the first batter. Then Jackson came in and got the last two outs. In this case, for a pitcher to be credited with a save he must pitch at least one full inning and protect a lead of three runs or fewer. Jackson didn't pitch a full inning. To be credited with a save if he doesn't work a full final inning he must enter the game with the tying run at bat, on base, or in the on-deck circle. The bases were empty when Jackson came in, and because he had a three-run lead, the first two batters he faced were no threat to a tie.

·················· **EARNED OR UNEARNED?** ··················

Q: After two outs in a given inning, and the inning is prolonged due to an error, are all subsequent runs in the given inning unearned? If so, are RBIs also forfeited? —*Dale Dieckman, Cleveland, OH* [4/14/79]

A: All the remaining runs that inning are unearned with respect to the defensive team. And if the same pitcher finishes the inning he wouldn't be charged for any of the runs. But if a new pitcher comes in and is responsible for putting men on base that eventually score without further error they will go against his personal record as earned runs.

But earned runs have nothing to do with RBIs. Every time a batter knocks in a run, give him credit for it.

Out of Left Field

Q: In view of the fact that some of the Tribe's pitchers have difficulty in holding runners on first, I would appreciate your thoughts on the idea of having the "pitcher" throw to the third baseman rather than pitching out on suspected steals. I feel that, if legal, it could benefit a team in several ways. For example, the throw from third to second is shorter than from home to second. Certainly it would psychologically work against the players who take advantage of certain Tribe pitchers. Would this ploy be legal?" —*B. F., Marion, OH* [7/26/77]

A: Unfortunately, it isn't. It is illegal to throw to an unoccupied base except for the purpose of making a play at that base.

It's too bad a lasso is illegal, too.

IMPOSSIBLE BALK

Q: Can a pitcher be called for a balk when there are no runners on base? I think it's impossible but a friend says otherwise.
—*John Pokky, Cleveland, OH* [10/17/82]

A: Tell your friend to give you an example of a balk with nobody on. He can't. It's impossible.

NOT THE RETIRING TYPE

Q: A friend and I have been arguing over the rule about how long a pitcher has to stay in the game. He states that a starting pitcher must stay in at least for one-third of an inning. I say that no pitcher, be he started or reliever, must face more than one batter. Please answer quickly as we have something more than pride riding on this. —*Henry M. Hartstein, Gambier, OH* [2/1/70]

A: You're right. A pitcher must remain in the game until the first batter he faces has completed his turn at bat. He does NOT have to pitch until he retires a batter. The batter may walk, get a hit, etc.

You mean money has greater value than pride?

······················ **ANY PART OF THE BALL** ····················

Q: Must the *entire* ball go over the plate to be in the strike zone? Also, must the entire ball be above the knees and below the batter's armpits to be in the strike zone? —*L. F. Lloyd, Tiffin, OH* [3/7/85]

A: If *any* part of the ball passes over *any* part of the strike zone, it's a strike. The strike zone is *any* part of the plate between the batter's armpits and the top of his knees during his normal stance. So if a teeny bit of the ball gets a teeny bit of the plate a teeny bit above the batter's knees, it's a strike. That is, if the umpire's eyes are that sharp.

······················ **WHAT A RELIEF** ····················

Q: If a new pitcher comes into a game with the count 3-and-2 on the batter and then strikes the batter out, who would get credit for the strikeout? —*Ronald Ashkenas, Lyndhurst, OH* [9/4/59]

A: The relief pitcher. But had the batter walked, instead of whiffed, the first pitcher would have been charged with the base on balls. Sounds fair, doesn't it.

······················ **EARNED OR UNEARNED?** ····················

Q: Pitcher X walks the first four batters he faces. Is the run that has scored *earned* or *unearned*? —*Ray* [8/22/75]

A: An earned run is one that the pitcher is responsible for. When he walks four men he certainly must bear the full responsibility.

But the pitcher probably will blame the umpire.

······················ **PITCH THEN SWITCH** ····················

Q: A friendly argument at a local bar about baseball. Suppose a pitcher in the major leagues throws right-handed. Can he throw the next pitch left-handed? In other words does it make a difference what hand a pitcher throws the ball with after he enters a game? Also, how about the batter? Can he switch at any time? —*George Hoffman, Crestline, OH* [3/29/69]

A: Both the batter and pitcher can switch sides and arms, respectively, on every pitch. So that this doesn't become a merry-go-round the batter is permitted to assume his position *after* the pitcher declares himself and once both men have taken their respective stances there can be no further changing for that pitch. But on the next pitch they can switch again.

If the hitter didn't have the last word there would be some men who would rather switch than pitch.

········· **FULL CREDIT** ·········

Q: Is the pitcher who pitches an entire rain-abbreviated baseball game given credit for a complete game? We know it's an official game but does it count as a completed game? —*E. F. Siegel, Akron, OH* [4/26/73]

A: Yes. He pitched a legally completed game, and gets full credit for going all the way. It's not his fault that it rained.

········· **THE RIGHT STEP** ·········

Q: Pitcher stands with pivot foot on the rubber, holding ball in pitching hand and behind his back. Runner is on third. Pitcher looks in for signal then glances at runner. Pitcher is facing batter. From this pitching position he sees runner coming too far off third and steps directly toward third, his hand coming from behind his back to throw to third base and not making contact with his gloved hand. His pivot foot remains in contact with the rubber while his free foot steps directly toward third base. This happened exactly as described and was called a balk. Should it have been? —*George Diadium, Painesville, OH* [7/12/69]

A: No. The pitcher did everything exactly right. From a set position the pitcher can throw to any occupied base as long as he steps directly toward it, which he did in this case.

In fact, it wouldn't have been a balk if the pitcher merely had faked a throw to third. Just so he steps in that direction.

If the umpire balks at this answer, he's being a mule about the whole thing.

OUT OF THIS WORLD

Q: If a pitcher comes into a game and gives up three runs without retiring a single batter and then is taken out, how do you figure out his earned run average since he hasn't pitched part of the inning? This question has been bothering me for a long time and I hope you can answer it. —*Larry Klasmier, Pittsburgh, PA* [5/17/80]

A: When the divisor is zero, the answer is too large to calculate and is known as infinity. In other words, it's up there with the sun and the stars and the sky. I hope you are no longer bothered. The pitcher is the one who must be.

A SARSAPARILLA BET

Q: I am having an argument with a friend. Would you please define an "earned run"? A sarsaparilla rides on your answer. —*Jim Kvasnicka, Garfield Heights, OH* [5/6/67]

A: It's one for which the pitcher is held accountable. "An earned run shall be charged every time a runner reaches home base by the aid of safe hits, sacrifice bunts, a sacrifice fly, stolen bases, putouts, fielder's choices, bases on balls, hit batters, balks or wild pitches before fielding chances have been offered to put out the offensive team."

Have you tried ginger beer?

HITTING PITCHER

Q: Regarding the designated hitter rule: If you had a pitcher who was a solid .280 hitter could he bat for himself as the DH? If he was knocked out of the box could he stay in the game as the DH? If the answer is yes to the first, I guess he would be the first man ever to be knocked out of half a game. —*Paul McCann, Twinsburg, OH* [2/24/76]

A: If the manager wants the pitcher to bat for himself he can't take advantage of the DH rule for that game. In other words the manager must designate before the game whether or not he intends to use a DH. If one isn't used at the start he can't use one later in the game.

So, to answer your questions directly. Yes, the pitcher can bat for himself. No, he can't stay in the game as a DH once he is knocked out of the box. He can move to another position, however, and maintain his same place in the batting order.

Of course, pitchers have moved from the rubber to other positions in the past, so your man wouldn't be the first to be half-knocked out.

······················· **FAULTY FIREMEN** ·······················

Q: In a game between the Mets and the Cubs last week Jerry Koosman pitched seven innings and Nino Espinosa pitched much less. Yet Espinosa was credited with the victory. How is this decided? —*Seth Armus, Toledo, OH* [4/17/77]

A: Koosman pitched seven innings and was leading, 6-3, when he was replaced. The two relief pitchers who followed, Bob Apodaca and Ray Sadecki, failed to hold the Cubs, who tied the score at 6. Espinosa, the Mets' third reliever, took over. The Mets scored two runs in the ninth to win, 8-6. Since he was the *pitcher of record* at the time the Cubs went ahead, he received credit for the victory. Once the score was tied after Koosman left, his contribution was nullified. He no longer could become the winner.

Sometimes relievers save games for the starters. And sometimes they can't even save themselves. Koosman was the victim of faulty firemen.

······················· **AWARDED ONE STAR** ·······················

Q: Here is a hypothetical but possible situation. First batter up strikes out but reaches first base as the third strike eludes the catcher for a passed ball. He is then caught stealing. Pitcher goes on to retire the final 26 batters without any of them reaching base. I figure this would be a no-hitter but would the pitcher be credited with a perfect game? —*David K. Catonzaro, Clearfield, PA* [7/24/77]

A: It certainly would be a no-hitter. It can't be a perfect game because a runner did reach first base. But in this case, I'm sure the record book will carry an asterisk to describe how close the pitcher came. He deserves at least one star.

IT'S OFFICIAL NOW

Q: This happened in our Little League game last summer. An outfielder, upon returning to his position in the field, stepped on the pitcher's rubber and threw a "warm-up" pitch to the catcher. Does this mean he is now the pitcher of record, even though no batter or umpire was nearby and no position change was announced to the official scorer? —*Philip Adams, Mansfield, OH* [1/14/89]

A: Yes. In Little League one warm-up constitutes official entry as a pitcher. Suppress the urge.

NO PITCH

Q: In a baseball game I played in last summer, our pitcher had just completed his warm-ups, the batter dug in and our pitcher, standing on the rubber, accidentally dropped the ball. The umpire called, "Ball one." A friend said the umpire should have called, "No pitch." What is the correct ruling? —*Don Hilt, Dover, OH* [1/11/89]

A: No pitch would be correct. With no one on base, dropping the ball isn't fooling anybody. By rule, it must be ignored. The ump merely should call, "Time," and allow the pitcher to get a grip on himself. With a runner on base, it's a balk if the pitcher drops the ball while on the rubber.

LEFT WITH NOTHING

Q: Nolan Ryan of the Astros is pitching against the New York Mets. Ryan is injured and leaves the game after the fourth inning with a 1-0 lead. Juan Agosto comes in and pitches four shutout innings. Dave Smith pitches the ninth as the Astros win, 1-0. Who gets credit for the win? —*Gary Willie, Medina, OH* [7/23/80]

A: Agosto is the winning pitcher and Smith receives credit for a save. Ryan is left with nothing, except for lowering his earned run average. A starting pitcher, in a nine-inning game, must go at least five innings to be credited with the victory.

THAT BALL IS ALIVE

Q: One man out, runner on first, tie score, and a left-handed pitcher on the mound. The pitcher begins his delivery toward home and the runner on first takes off on a gamble steal. The pitcher, seeing the runner break, throws the ball wild past the first baseman and into the right-field corner. However, in doing so he balked. The third base umpire immediately yelled, "Balk." Meanwhile, the runner races around the bases and scores. The team in the field argued that the umpire had killed the ball when the "balk" call was made. The argument was disallowed and the run was allowed. Were the umpires correct?
—*Gary Spizer, West Chester, PA* [3/6/98]

A: Yes. Once the runner reaches the base to which he was entitled because of the balk he can continue to run. The ball isn't dead until the entire play is concluded. If the runner had been tagged out at the plate, I'll bet the defensive team wouldn't have complained.

FOREIGN SUBSTANCES

Q: Occasionally, while watching baseball on television I see leather thongs hanging from the pitcher's glove. Why isn't this illegal, since it could be quite disconcerting to the batter?
—*Alice Millson, East Haven, CT* [4/10/98]

A: It is illegal if the umpire thinks if it is a distraction. The ump will order the pitcher to get another glove or cut off the strings or thongs. If a batter complains about the hanging pieces of leather, the ump will force their removal immediately. Umpires are advised to consider anything that isn't a necessary part of the glove or that is a distraction a "foreign substance," which is verboten.

ISN'T THAT A BALK?

Q: During a recent high school game this play occurred. No outs, runner on third. Pitcher comes to a set position. As pitcher starts to pitch, batter steps out of batter's box. Pitcher stops. Umpire didn't call anything. My friends insisted he should have called a balk. I said I thought he did the right thing. We have a soda riding on your answer. —*Jerry Perona, Northfield, OH* [6/4/78]

A: The umpire was absolutely correct and so are you. Both the pitcher and batter have violated the rule. Therefore, the umpire merely should call time and have both start from scratch. It would be totally wrong to call a balk.

The purpose of the balk rule is to prevent the pitcher from fooling the runner. It doesn't give the batter the right to fool the pitcher.

OFF-STRIDE

Q: Supposing there was a pitcher who possessed true ambidexterity (could pitch right- and left-handed), would he be permitted to do so in a game? If so, would he have to notify the umpire when changing? Would you agree that such a pitcher might be able to throw the batter off-stride? —*Paddy Lebato, Cleveland, OH* [2/11/60]

A: It is perfectly legal for a pitcher to use either arm in delivering the ball and he can alternate on each pitch, if he so wishes, without notifying the umpire. But he must assume the correct pitcher's position on the mound before each delivery and in no way commit a balk motion. For example, he couldn't throw with his gloved hand, nor could he switch the ball from one hand to the other in the middle of his windup.

My opinion is that such switching would throw the pitcher off-stride more than it would the hitter.

UNCHANGED COUNT

Q: When a relief pitcher takes over for the starting pitcher on a batter who has one or more strikes, does the strike count go down to zero? We think this is true, but a nonbeliever bet us otherwise. —*Craig Tellard, Mansfield, OH* [8/24/75]

A: The count remains unchanged when a pitching change is made. It would be unfair otherwise and, therefore, you lose to the non-believer.

········· **BALK AND INTERFERENCE** ·········

Q: There is a runner on third base. The suicide squeeze is on. The catcher, in his haste to get the pitched ball, jumps in front of the plate to tag the runner and does so before the batter can swing. The umpire awards the batter first base for catcher's interference. Also, he allows the runner from third to score, charging a balk on the play. Was this the correct call? —*Rob Wilson, Mansfield, OH* [1/3/98]

A: Yes. Whenever the catcher leaves his box too soon while a runner is on base, the pitcher is charged with a balk. That allows the runner to score. The batter goes to first because the catcher interfered with his opportunity to swing. Thus, you have a balk and interference on the same play.

········· **PITCHING FROM OFF THE RUBBER** ·········

Q: Bases loaded, nobody out. Pitcher steps off the rubber and throws to the plate. The runner on third was *not* trying for home. Is this an illegal pitch and, therefore, a balk and a ball to the batter? Or is this a balk because the pitcher threw to an unoccupied base? If the batter had hit the pitch, would he have been out for the interference? In the game which I saw it was not obvious to the batter that the pitcher had stepped off the rubber. —*Phil Richardson, Lorain, OH* [11/28/98]

A: It's an illegal pitch, therefore a balk. All runners advance one base, but the count on the batter is unchanged. If the runner from third had been trying to steal home the pitcher could have legally backed off the rubber. But since there was no reason for him to do so, he was committing a balk by pitching with his foot off the rubber. If the batter swung at the pitch and reached first safely and all other runners advanced at least one base, the balk would be forgotten. But if the batter missed the pitch or made an out, the balk would prevail. The pitcher fooled nobody but himself.

DEAD BALL ON A BALK?

Q: The Yanks' Rickey Henderson is on first base. The Rangers' Charley Hough throws over to keep him close to the bag. As Hough makes the move toward first a balk is called. Hough throws the ball over the first baseman's head. Henderson circles the bases and scores. The umpire said the run counts. How can this be? Isn't the ball dead on a balk? —*Mike Maturi, Lorain, OH* [9/24/88]

A: There are two exceptions. On a balk the ball remains alive if the batter hits it and all runners, including the batter, advance at least one base. The ball also remains alive if the pitcher makes a wild throw either to a base or to the plate. In that case, the runners can try to advance beyond the base they would have been awarded on the balk. That's why Henderson was allowed to run and score.

APPEAL OR BALK?

Q: Hot Stove League. Batter hit a ground-rule double and missed first base. Pitcher stood on rubber with ball in hand and ump said, "Play ball." Pitcher threw to first by stepping directly toward the base. Ump said balk for throwing to an unoccupied base. My question: Was he right? I noticed a similar play in the majors except that the pitcher stepped back off the rubber before throwing to an unoccupied base. Please discuss. —*Paul E. Lucas, Akron, OH* [8/1/78]

A: Many umpires are confused by this rule and the book could clarify this apparent inconsistency. Nevertheless, it *is* legal for the pitcher to throw to an unoccupied base for the purpose of making an appeal. It is not a balk. The pitcher would be wise to inform the umpire in advance that he is going to appeal, then get on the rubber and throw to the base. But if the appeal is obvious, it's tantamount to an announcement.

Whether the pitcher steps directly to the base from the rubber or backs off the rubber and then throws made no difference with respect to the appeal. Both ways are legal.

However, the pitcher should be advised that if he throws directly from the rubber he's still a pitcher, and if he happens to throw the ball into the stands, the runner can advance only one base. But when he backs off he becomes an infielder and a wild throw would give the runner two bases.

Just thought I would give you a tip.

················· **STRETCHING THE RULES** ·················

Q: There are runners on first and third. Left-handed pitcher goes into his stretch. Runner on first breaks for second and the pitcher watches him going all the way to second without making any move to home or to the base. After the runner rounds second, the pitcher delivers ball to the plate and the batter fouls it off. Does the runner stay at second or return to first? I ruled that he stays on second because the base was made before he attempted to deliver the pitcher the batter. —*John Leonbruno, Fairport Harbor, OH* [5/21/63]

A: You were wrong. The runner must return to first base just as he would on any other foul ball. The pitch begins the moment the pitcher starts his stretch.

Next time, if you want to penalize the pitcher, charge him the price of admission for being a spectator.

················· **NEW ROLE FOR PITCHER** ·················

Q: I need two answers to satisfy my son-in-law. One—May a pitcher fake a throw to first base if he is not on the rubber? Two—Runner on first, pitcher takes his stretch. He turns to throw to first. Runner breaks for second. Must the pitcher throw to first? —*Jim Hanel, Canton, OH* [5/29/77]

A: If the pitcher is off the rubber he no longer is considered a pitcher. He is the same as any other fielder. Therefore he can fake a throw to first base.

On your second question the pitcher doesn't have to throw to first if the runner is breaking for second. After turning to first he can throw to second.

Hope this satisfies your son-in-law—and you.

················· **WILD PITCHER** ·················

Q: In baseball, what's the ruling: A man is on first base. The pitcher takes his stretch, looks to first base, *takes his foot off the rubber*, then throws to first base to get the runner. The ball is overthrown and goes into the stands. How many bases is the runner on first awarded? —*William Winky, Maple Heights, OH* [5/31/70]

A: The instant the pitcher backs off the rubber, like magic, he *becomes an infielder* and is no longer considered a pitcher. Thus the wild throw was made by an infielder in this case. The runner is awarded two bases. If the pitcher had made the wild throw without backing off the rubber he would have remained a pitcher and the runner would have been given only one base.

In summary, the runner goes to third on the play you describe. The pitcher can get back on the rubber and become a pitcher again.

5

Safe or Out?

······················· **IT'S WRITTEN, ALL RIGHT** ·····················

Q: Have you ever heard of the supposedly "unwritten rule" in baseball where the runner is given the edge on any play that may appear to be a tie, such as the runner and the ball getting to the base at the same time. Does the runner get the advantage or is there no such thing as a tie in baseball? I'm referring to force plays in particular. —*Ken Wohlgemuth, Euclid, OH* [7/5/71]

A: *The written rule* states that for a runner to be declared out the ball must get to the base *before* he does. Therefore, if they both get there at the same time the runner has to be safe. Hence, the expression "tie favor the runner" is not an unwritten rule. It's real. Hope this doesn't make you fit to be tied.

·························· **WASTED ENERGY** ·························

Q: A batter has two strikes on him. He swings at the next pitch which is way inside and the ball hits him. The ball hits the ground and rolls away. Can the batter run to first base? —*B. J., Rocky River, OH* [3/3/61]

A: If he does he'll merely be wasting energy. The ball is dead as soon as it hits him. He's out because he struck out. He may also be knocked out.

·························· **SAFE AT HOME** ·························

Q: Runner on third base steals home. The ball is thrown to the catcher and the runner jumped over the catcher and hit home plate and was not tagged by the catcher. The umpire called him safe and everybody thinks he should have been called out. Why did the ump call him safe? If the runner was not out of line and he was on the plate and he was not tagged, is that reason enough for him to be safe? —*Charles Perell, Ferrell, PA* [9/22/79]

A: I can't think of a better reason. He reached home safely. That's why he was called safe. As a matter of fact, judging from your description, the catcher might have stepped in front of the plate to get the pitch. I am assuming this because the runner had to jump over him. If the catcher took the pitch in front of the plate, this would be a balk and interference. The runner would be awarded home and the batter would be sent to first. In any event, he's safe.

TAG HOME

Q: Bases are loaded with two outs and two strikes against the batter. A third strike is called. The catcher drops the ball and throws to first base. Instead, can the catcher simply touch home plate for a force out against the runner on third? Or must the catcher tag the batter or throw to first? —*Marshall Graves, New Philadelphia, OH* [4/22/88]

A: He can tag home. In fact, he should. Why risk a throw to first when home plate is right there?

ANY PART OF THE BODY

Q: This happened while I was playing first base this summer. Bottom of the ninth, two outs, nobody on and we're winning 4-1. The batter hits a hard grounder to the second baseman. He picks it up and the throw slips out of his hand and lands between first and second. I run over, pick it up, and see no one is covering first. I run to the base, slide head first, arm stretched out, ball in hand and tag the base before the runner touches it. The umpire calls the runner safe, saying I made an illegal tag. Is the umpire right or should he go back to umpiring school? —*Rick Pfaff, Willard, OH* [11/4/89]

A: He needs at least one more class. The batter-runner should have been called out. As long as you are holding the ball securely, you can tag the base with any part of your body, and certainly with the ball. Just so the tag beats the runner.

HOLD ON TIGHT

Q: If a runner is tagged by a defensive player and the defensive player loses the ball but a teammate grabs it before the ball hits the ground, is the runner safe or out? —*Mike Howell, Pikeville, NC* [8/31/80]

A: The runner is safe. The tagger must hold the ball securely. The instant he failed to do so the runner was safe. The attempted rescue by his teammates was in vain.

OUT AND OUT

Q: One out, runner on first. A left-handed batter is up and he hits a line drive that crashes into the face of the runner on first while he is standing on the base and the ball then rolls into the dugout. The umpire puts the runners on first and second. Is this a judgment call? —*Alex Patterson, West Chester, PA* [9/26/98]

A: No. In baseball the runner is out—perhaps in this case literally. The base is not an island of safety. The ball is dead immediately and the batter is awarded first base and credited with a single.

Out of Left Field

Q: A runner is stealing second. His slide is short, so he quickly takes off his helmet and reaches the base with it. Just his helmet touches the base, not his hand, and he is tagged while in this position. Safe or out? —*Oscar Freund, Mansfield, OH* [12/13/06]

A: He's out. A player isn't allowed to gain any advantage by using detached equipment.

A FOUL SPLIT

Q: It's the last game of the regular season. The Red Sox and Yankees are tied for first place. It's the bottom of the ninth, with two outs. The score is tied 3-3. Mike Greenwell is up. Dave

Righetti releases a 3-2 pitch. Greenwell hits a long fly straight down the right-field foul line. The ball hits the foul pole and splits in half, one part going into the seats in foul territory and the other half goes fair. Would the Sox be in the playoffs or is this just another foul ball? —*Aron Willey, Mansfield, OH* [7/27/88]

A: The instant the ball hits the foul pole it's a home run. Game over. Red Sox win. No halfway about it.

ONE, TWO, THREE

Q: In a Little League game the opposing team thought there were three outs but there weren't. A kid on my team assumed there were three outs, too, but there were only two. The manager of the other team told their players there were only two outs and told them to tag our runner who was heading to the dugout. He ran back to second base and was tagged out before he got there. The umpire called him out. Was he correct? —*Jason Aspina, New Philadelphia, OH* [7/1/88]

A: Yes. All the players should know—and are responsible for knowing—how many outs there are. It's not that tough to count up to three.

STILL IN PLAY

Q: Batter gets a base on balls and breaks for second base, where a play is made on him. Is he entitled only to first base and must he stop there? —*Fred Heinlen, Shaker Heights, OH* [7/20/75]

A: The ball remains in play on a base on balls. The batter can try for as many bases as his daring dictates. As baseball coach at Shaker, Fred, I am sure you knew the answer. You must be trying to convince somebody who doesn't believe.

THROW IT INTO REVERSE

Q: There is a runner on first. The batter hits a long fly to right that drops in the corner. As the runner who was on first rounds third he misses the bag. Meanwhile the batter touches third. The runner ahead of him, realizing he missed third, goes back to tag it and the batter backs up so they don't pass. Then they continue home. Is the batter out or safe? —*Mike Timko* [8/10/75]

A: If the batter, after backing up, touched third again on his way to the plate, his procedure was perfectly proper and both runs count. Fortunately, the batter was able to throw himself into reverse gear without getting stuck.

.... **KICK IT AROUND** ....

Q: This happened in a recent softball game. There is a man on second, one out. The batter hits a line drive toward the pitcher. The pitcher can't hang onto the ball. It goes off his glove and hits the runner on his way toward third. The ball strikes the runner in the leg and he unintentionally kicks it into foul territory. I say the runner is safe and can have all the bases he can get, but others say the runner is out. Please clear up the argument. —*R. Garth, Euclid, OH* [5/10/70]

A: Inasmuch as the ball first was touched by the pitcher and the kicking by the runner was unintentional the ball remains in play. The runner is *not* out and he can keep on running.
Tell those who disagree to kick that around.

.... **THE RULE SAYS . . .** ....

Q: Here's a situation for you to call: Runner on first and second, two outs. The batter hits a grounder to the shortstop and the runner on second circles behind the fielder. The ball goes through the shortstop's legs—he doesn't touch it—and hits the runner advancing to third. Is he safe or out, and why?
—*A. Georgalas, Niles, OH* [7/20/75]

A: The runner is safe because the fielder had his chance to field the ball. The ball remains in play and the fact that it touched the runner is ignored. Why? Because Rule 5.09f says so.

.... **FIELDING A SOFTBALL** ....

Q: Recently in an answer to Frank Loves, of Fairview Park, pertaining to a batted ball going through an infielder, hitting the runner behind him while another infielder was behind the runner ready to field the ball, you said that since the ball passed an infielder the runner is safe. I disagree. As long as another infielder has a chance to make a play on the ball the batter is out. Check the softball rules. —*Glenn K. Cadiou, Perry, OH* [9/2/75]

A: Since Mr. Love's question did not mention softball I assumed he was referring to baseball and the answer I gave him was correct. But I must admit had he specified softball I would have given him the wrong answer. In softball you are right and I would have been wrong. If another infielder has a chance to make a play on a ball that hits a runner *after* passing a fellow infielder the runner is *out*. I think this is a ridiculous rule. Example: Third baseman is playing up. Ball goes through his legs untouched, hits runner who is going to third, thus preventing shortstop behind him from making a play. In softball the runner is out *even if the third baseman is charged with an error on the play*. Isn't that awful? But that's what the softball rulemakers decided this year and I'm glad Mr. Cadiou called my attention to it.

INFIELD FLY MUFF

Q: Please answer this one for me. Less than two outs, runners on first and second. Batter hits a pop fly to the infield. Umpire calls "infield fly." Shortstop and second baseman each think the other is going to catch the ball. It falls untouched about two feet from the base and bounces into runner who is standing on second. Is runner on second safe or out? This is baseball, not softball. —*Joseph A. Forbes* [1/30/77]

A: Safe. In baseball the only time a runner hit by a batted ball isn't out is when he is standing on the base during an infield fly situation. Even if he were hit on the head he'd be safe, although perhaps out—knocked out.

DAD'S GOT IT

Q: A baseball question: Man on second base. A pop-up in the infield. Nobody out. The infielders call each other off the ball and it strikes the runner on the fly while he is standing on the base. Is the runner out or safe? Consensus around here is that he is safe and the "Dad" says he's out. —*Second Floor, Stewart Hall, Kent State University, Kent, OH* [2/16/75]

A: Always listen to "Dad." The runner is out. In baseball the base is not an island of safety except during an infield fly situation. But in your example, the infield fly rule isn't in effect since you don't have runners on *first and second*. On your play, the runner is out, the ball is dead, the batter gets first base and is credited with a hit.

If the discussion had been about softball, you would have been right and "Dad" would have been wrong, for in softball the base *is* an island of safety.

JUST ONE TIME

Q: Is it possible to score a run after three outs? I know you had this in your column before, but would you please repeat it as no one I talk to believes it is legally possible. Please reveal your source of information. —*Tex Rickard, Sandusky, OH* [5/29/59]

A: According to the rules book, it is impossible to score a run after three outs, but in this *one* instance the official rules committee makes an exception: Suppose there are two outs and the bases are filled. The batter draws a base on balls, forcing the runner on third to come home. He does so slowly. Meanwhile, the runner going from second to third, tags third, steps beyond it, and is picked off for the third out *before* the preceding runner tags home plate. Nevertheless, he is entitled to home and when he does touch the plate the run scores.

GET IT, GRAB IT

Q: Would you please clarify the rule on a foul tip being caught on the third strike. One rules book says if a foul tip hits the mitt or bare hand and goes against the chest protector or mask and is caught, it's a strike. I was under the impression that a foul tip must be caught cleanly and not trapped or caught, even though it hits the glove first. I'm talking about the major league rule. —*Ralph Pappada, Niles, OH* [5/23/71]

A: It's illegal to use the protector, mask, cap, or any part of the uniform as a trap. This means a player can't make a basket out of his blouse and catch the ball in it, or catch it in his cap or mask, or make a "cradle" out of his protector and use it as a net. But it's perfectly legal to catch a ball *against* a uniform.

Thus, a player can trap the ball against his jersey, or mask or protector, and if he then is able to transfer it securely into his hand or glove it becomes a catch.

Now, as for a foul tip we have one variation. A foul tip, by definition, must go "sharp and direct" to the catcher's hands or glove. Thus, if it first hits his protector mask it no longer is a foul tip and *can't* be caught. It simply becomes a foul ball and the batter remains at bat. But if it *first* hits his glove or hand, it is a foul tip and until it hits the ground. Therefore, if after touching the glove it then hits his protector or mask and is caught against either one as explained in the above paragraph, or rebounds from either one and is caught, it becomes a legally caught foul tip and would be the third strike.

Got it? Then grab it.

·························· **TAGGED BAT** ··························

Q: There is nothing riding on this answer. It's not a matter of life or death—just plain curiosity. Say a batter is running to first base with the bat in both hands and the fielder tagged the bat. Would the runner be safe or out? —*C. Campanaro* [2/21/65]

A: He's out. The bat becomes part of him when he holds it, so it's a legal tag. A batter who carries a bat to first base is batty.

·················· **Out of Left Field** ··················

Q: My eight-year-old son, Bryan, who is fond of asking me bizarre questions, asked this one today: Buddy Bell pulls a long drive over the stadium fence, but due to a freakish bounce the ball hops back over the fence into the playing field and the startled left fielder holds equally startled Bell at second. Is it a home run or ground, rule double? I advised Bryan that the play couldn't happen, but if it did, Bell would get a homer. Was I right on both scores? —*Bruce J. Havighurst, Cleveland, OH* [6/20/76]

A: I don't know if such a bounce is possible, but the reason umpires run to the outfield on long drives is to follow the flight of the ball. Once it goes over the fence and hits something on the other side, it's a homer, no matter how or where it bounces afterward. So you're right. But if Bryan keeps coming at you, I'd suggest you buy a rules book.

·················· **READY TO PLAY** ·······················

Q: The batter hits a double and after he slides safely into second he calls time to brush himself off. The umpire acknowledges the request. When the runner indicates he is ready, the umpire, without making sure that the pitcher has the ball, calls, "Play." The runner leads off second and is tagged by the second baseman who has the ball.

I know this is wrong because play can not be resumed until the pitcher has the ball *on the rubber*. What should be the correct handling of this erroneous call by the umpire?
—*Ross W. McPherson, Jr., Lyndhurst, OH* [5/14/61]

A: The umpire's announcement of "Play" merely meant that the runner was ready and that play would resume when the pitcher got the ball on the rubber and assumed pitching position. The runner could *not* be tagged out until then.

The umpire should have said, after the tag, "Forget it. We're ready to play, but the ball is still dead and will be until the pitcher gets it. You can't tag a man out while the ball is dead."

A good umpire always knows what to say, and if you call 'em right you rarely have to say much.

·················· **HONEST, IT'S LEGAL** ·····················

Q: Is it an out or a home run—and does the position of the glove in relation to the stands or fence have any bearing on the decision—when an outfielder leaps, catches the ball, and then falls over the fence or into the stands? —*Santo Giardino, Sandusky, OH* [6/6/75]

A: It's an out if the fielder does not drop the ball after he lands. The position of the glove at the time of the catch is of no consequence. It can be way over the fence when he makes the catch.

This over-the-fence catch is one players and fans don't want to believe. It comes in at least 20 times a year. Honest, it's a legal catch. Really, truly. No kidding.

······················· **EVERYBODY RUNS** ························

Q: Is a base runner out if he runs into a batted ball that has been deflected off the pitcher or any other defensive fielder? If not out, and he accidentally kicks the ball into outfield foul territory, how far can he and the other base runners advance?
—*Jack Price, Rocky River, OH* [6/14/60]

A: The base runner is not out in the play you describe, since the ball touched a defensive player *before* it hit the runner. If, in the umpire's judgment, the ball was accidentally kicked, as you say, it is in play and everybody runs.

But if the kicking is judged intentional, the runner is out and the ball is dead. This isn't soccer, you know.

····················· **THAT'S INTERFERENCE** ·····················

Q: Team A is at bat with the bases loaded, two out and a three-two count on the batter. On the payoff pitch, with the runners traveling, the batter hits a pop-up directly over home plate. The catcher then gets up, stands on home, and waits for the ball to come down. Meanwhile the runner from third comes sliding into home and knocks the catcher off his feet. With runner's foot already home, the ball comes down and hits his hand in foul territory. How would you rule this play? —*Richard Fishman, S. Euclid, OH* [5/5/67]

A: The runner *must* avoid a fielder attempting to field a batted ball. I rule the runner out for interference. I would rule on this play without hesitation.

························ **LITTLE BALL** ·························

Q: A batter hits a ball which hits a runner going from first to second. What is the batter credited with? Also, a runner who was on third base at the time scores on the play. Does the run count if the out is not the third out? —*Tom Wolfe, Willard, OH* [5/5/67]

A: The batter whose ball hit the runner receives credit for a base hit and he is awarded first base. The runner is out. The ball is dead; therefore, no runs can score on this play. The runner who was on third must return to that base.

And all because a little ball hit a great big runner.

FUN IN FOUL TERRITORY

Q: If a player in the major leagues jumped into the stands (in foul territory) or jumped over the fence (in fair territory) and caught a fly ball while his feet were inside the stands or over the fence, is the batter out? —*Richard P. Beattie, Willowick, OH* [8/4/70]

A: If the fielder makes the catch before landing in the stands or before his feet touch the ground on the other side of the fence the batter is out.

Of course, the fielder must continue to hold the ball after landing. If he drops it the batter is safe and the acrobatics are a flop.

ADVANCE ONE

Q: On a long drive toward the stands, the left fielder races toward the wall, leaps and catches the ball and then falls into the stands. There is one out and a runner on second. What's the ruling? —*Larry Sadowski, Warren, OH* [3/16/91]

A: If the fielder holds onto the ball after landing on the other side of the wall, the batter is out and the ball is dead. All runners advance one base, so the runner from second, after tagging out, goes to third.

WORLDS IN COLLISION

Q: This happened in one of our pick-up softball games: The batter lifts a pop fly down the first-base line. Attempting to make the catch the pitcher charges off the mound with his eyes focused on the ball in flight. The batter makes a mad dash for the first base and the two collide about halfway to the bag and directly in the baseline. They are sprawled out on the ground with the ball landing not far away. Is the batter automatically out, or is he awarded first base? Does play continue? —*Jeff Herman, Mentor, OH* [3/6/99]

A: The batter-runner is out and the ball is dead immediately. If any other runners are on base they must stay put. A runner must avoid a fielder attempting to field a batted ball. This runner was out twice—physically and mentally.

······················ **NO INTERFERENCE** ······················

Q: This recently happened in my slow-pitch softball league: Runners on first and second, two outs. I hit the ball up the middle, the pitcher deflects it and it hits the runner going from second to third. The umpire ruled the runner was out for interfering with the ball. Was this the correct call? —*Darren Brant, Dover, OH* [9/24/88]

A: No. Since the ball was first touched by another player the ball should have remained in play. The fact that it hit the runner should have been disregarded. No interference.

······················ **OUT IN THE DUGOUT** ······················

Q: In a recent game our pitcher hit a batter. The batter went toward first base but stopped just short of the base and never touched it. A runner was put in his place. The hit batter was not injured in any way that would have prevented him from continuing to first base. We appealed and the umpire said he did not have to tag first. Was this the proper call? —*C. C., Wickliffe, OH* [8/1/85]

A: No. The umpire should have called the batter out when he went into the dugout. No appeal was necessary. Unless the batter becomes incapacitated, he must tag first base before he is replaced by a pinch runner.

······················ **THE INNING IS OVER** ······················

Q: Runners are on first and second, with one out. The batter hits a ground ball to shortstop, a perfect double play ball, but the runner on his way to third lets the ball hit him. The umpire rules that the runner *intentionally* stopped so the ball would hit him, thereby preventing the double play. If so, what would the umpire's decision be? —*Daniel Paller, Cleveland Heights, OH* [7/7/68]

A: The runner going to third is out. So is the batter. The inning is over. The runner attempting to break up the double play double-crossed himself.

········· **BODY WORKS** ·········

Q: This happened to me last summer and everyone I tell agrees with me except the umpire. There are runners on first and second base. I am playing third base. The batter hits a grounder to me. It takes an odd bounce and goes into foul territory. I dive for the ball and pick it up with my bare hand. While the ball is in my bare hand I place my glove hand on third base before the runner gets there. I say the runner is out because it's a force play. The umpire ruled safe because the ball was not in my glove hand. Control of the ball was not the issue because I held the ball up, and securely, in my bare hand. Was I right or the umpire? —*Ron Schwartz, Vermilion, OH* [3/7/85]

A: The runner should have been called out. The ump blew it. When the glove is on the hand, it is considered part of the body. And on a force play, it is legal to touch the base with any part of your body. Even your nose.

········· **FAN INTERFERENCE?** ·········

Q: In the second game of the Decoration Day doubleheader, in the last of the ninth, Curt Blefary hit a fly ball to Rocky Colavito, and as he went back to catch the ball the fans started throwing popcorn boxes and scorecards at Rocky to distract him. If he would have been hit by a scorecard, and he took his eye off the ball to see what happened, and the ball dropped safely, would they call the batter out for the fan's interference or would it be a hit? —*Bob Lester, Cleveland, OH* [6/4/67]

A: If, in the umpire's judgment, the fan's scorecard caused Rocky to miss the ball the batter would be called out. And the fan would be wise to get out, too. The gendarmes and Rocky would be chasing him.

········· **CLOSE TO THE CHEST** ·········

Q: If a player catches a ball and he feels it's going to slip out of his glove, can he hold it against his chest? And if he does, would it still be an out? —*Jay Rubinberg, Shaker Heights, OH* [6/16/63]

A: Yes, providing he doesn't have a slippery chest.

6

For the Defense

Questions about Fielding

························· **THROWN GLOVE** ·······················

Q: Indians 0, Yankees 0, bottom of the ninth, two outs, and the bases empty. Jim Thome hits a missile that's headed for the right field bleachers. At the last second Paul O'Neill, Yankee's right fielder, throws his glove into the air, knocking the ball down before it goes over the wall. The glove and the ball land on the warning track. O'Neill picks up the ball and fires it into second base where a stunned Thome is tagged out. What's the call? —*Brad Burton, North Ridgeville, OH; Jason Wright, Lorain, OH* [11/7/98]

A: Thome certainly is not out. By rule he is awarded a triple. This doesn't seem fair, since he clearly would have had a home run if O'Neill hadn't been such a crack glove thrower. I don't think the rulemakers ever anticipated an illegal act preventing an obvious homer. Therefore, in this case, I can see the umpire invoking rule 9.01(c) which gives him the right to make whatever call he thinks is fair and proper and, in this case, awarding Thome the homer. I think it would stand up if the Yanks protested. Otherwise fielders, having nothing to lose, would be throwing gloves every time they saw a ball flying out of the park. In any event, Thome, by rule, would at least get a triple.

CRY FOUL

Q: Here's one for you. Runner on third base. The Red Sox's Roger Clemens is facing the Indians' Brook Jacoby. As Clemens winds up, the runner on third breaks for the plate. Jacoby swings and hits a one-hopper toward the mound. The ball hits the rubber and bounds high in the air toward first base and hits Jacoby, who is running in foul territory, on the helmet. The ball then rolls fair. It is picked up by Clemens, who throws to first to beat Jacoby. Meanwhile, the runner has scored. What's the ruling? —*Jeff Golich, Mansfield, OH* [4/13/91]

A: Foul ball. The runner returns to third and Jacoby is still at bat. That was too easy. Come up with a harder one.

FAIR OR FOUL?

Q: A batted ball hits the first base bag, bounces up, hits the first baseman's glove and rolls into foul territory. Is this fair? —*Mark Nagy, Brunswick, OH* [6/26/77]

A: Absolutely. The base is in fair territory. Once it hit the base it had to be a fair ball no matter what happened to it afterward. If the ump didn't call it fair, he made a foul call. Ouch.

THERE'S A CATCH

Q: Let's say the bases are loaded, with two out. A ball is hit sharply to center field. The center field gets a bad jump. As he runs up to catch the ball his glove falls off. He runs hard and catches the ball with his *bare hands*. His momentum then causes him to do a belly slide. As he slides, the ball also slides with him, but he is still holding the ball cleanly. The ball touches the ground as he slides. Would it be a trap or a catch? —*Barb Matthes, Independence, OH* [1/20/73]

A: This is a legal catch. The ball was caught in the air and held securely after the fielder hit the ground. The other team may feel trapped because it's the third out and all those potential runs died on the bases.

·············· **PHANTOM TAGS** ··············

Q: Does either the second baseman or shortstop have to touch second base before making a double play? —*J. L. Verne, Columbus, OH* [9/19/76]

A: I presume you're talking about the double play that starts by a force at second. If so, *yes*, the bag *must* be touched. Some umpires appear to let the pivot man get away with a phantom touch on occasion. When they do, they're wrong. Generally the instant replays show the pivot man actually did touch the base while in possession of the ball, *but not always.*

Phantoms belong in haunted houses, not in ballparks.

·············· **THE EASY WAY OUT** ··············

Q: Would you please straighten out a few of us at the office on a baseball question? There are three on the sacks and two outs. The count on the batter is three balls and two strikes. On the next pitch the batter swings and misses the ball completely, but the catcher drops the third strike. What play does the catcher have? —*Joseph Bogacki, Broadview Heights, OH* [8/21/77]

A: He had three possible plays. He can try to tag the batter, or he can throw to first base, or he can tag home plate for the force out.

I'd tag home. It's the easiest and safest. Beside, I'm a home boy.

·············· **A LONG STRIKE** ··············

Q: A batter hits a long fly. The outfielder goes toward the stands and while he is in fair territory the ball bounces off his glove and into the stands in foul territory. Is this a ground-rule double or a home run? —*Wendell Hurst, Warren, OH* [5/3/91]

A: If the ball itself was in fair territory when first touched, it's a fair ball. Since it caromed off the glove and into the stands in foul territory, it's a ground-rule double. It doesn't make any difference, however, where the fielder is standing when he touches the ball. The position of the ball is all that matters. If the fielder is in fair territory, and he reaches across the line and touches the ball, it's a foul ball and it becomes just a long strike.

Out of Left Field

Q: A purely hypothetical situation: The batter is up; here comes the pitch; the batter swings, connects, and *smashes the ball to smithereens.* Is this considered a strike or a home run?
—*Jeane Hendersen, Cleveland, OH* [10/25/77]

A: It would be neither if Smithereens fields the ball cleanly and throws the batter out.

Seriously, although I don't know how serious one can get about your imaginative question, the rules book does provide for normal ripping of the ball. If it becomes partially apart it is in play until the play is completed. If it disintegrates totally, as you describe, I'd call it no play, not even a strike.

I don't advise playing with the Atom Ball.

FOUL ERRORS

Q: Box seat tickets ride on this one. A friend says that under no circumstances can a fielder be charged with an error on a foul ball. I say that it's a judgment call by the official scorer. Please advise. —*Jim Wagnon, Warren, OH* [5/15/91]

A: Your friend deserves to lose for making such a foolish statement. When a fielder drops a fly, fair or foul, that should be caught with ordinary effort and thus prolongs the life of the batter, he must be charged with an error, with one exception. When there is a runner on third base and the fielder purposely drops a foul fly to prevent him from scoring after the catch, no error will be charged.

NO WAY, JOSE

Q: It's the bottom of the ninth, the score is tied and there are two outs. The Athletics are playing the Indians in Oakland. Mark McGwire is batting while Jose Canseco is on third. McGwire hits a slow roller to Felix Fermin at short and Canseco heads home. The A's batboy goes in front of the plate to get the bat. Fermin throws home. The batboy is clearly in the way of Canseco sliding home. Sandy Alomar tags him before he can touch the plate. Is he out? —*Kevin Selm, Mansfield, OH* [6/16/90]

A: Yes. There was no interference or obstruction by the Indians. Canseco was blocked by an authorized member of the A's. Tough luck. Batboys are under orders not to go near a bat until the play is entirely over.

···················· WHERE'S THE BALL? ····················

Q: In a recent slo-pitch game one of our batters hit a fly ball down the left field line. The left fielder gave chase and touched the ball with her glove. At the time she touched the ball she was in fair territory and the ball was in foul territory. Is it fair or foul ball? I say it is a fair ball because the fielder was standing in fair territory, but the umpire called it a foul ball. He said it doesn't matter where the fielder is, but where the ball is. Who is right? It cost us a couple of runs. —*Marcia Shutty, Euclid* [7/4/85]

A: You lost those runs legitimately. The umpire was right. The position of the ball at the time it is touched is the determining factor. Next time you see the ump, tell him he was right. He knows, but he'll appreciate hearing it from you.

···················· FORCED AT THIRD ····················

Q: Bases loaded, nobody out. A ground ball is hit to the third baseman. The runner on third doesn't move. The third base-man turns and tags the runner on third. He sees the runner from second coming so he steps on the bag. The umpire ruled that the runner did not have to move off third, so he counted out only the runner who was approaching from second. Was he right? —*Felix Mataya, Niles, OH* [6/15/89]

A: No. The third baseman perfectly executed a double play. The runner on third was forced to advance on the ground ball. He didn't, therefore was out when tagged. The runner from second was forced at third when the third baseman stepped on the bag.

BUNT-ABILITY

Q: This play occurred in a recent Indians-White Sox game in Chicago. The Indians had runners on first and second with none out. The Indians' batter, attempting a sacrifice bunt, popped the ball about eight feet in the air directly at the pitcher. The pitcher let the ball drop without touching it, then picked it up and began an easy third-to-second double play because the runners had retreated to first and second when they saw the ball was popped up. Shouldn't the umpires have called an "infield fly" on this play to protect the runners? —*Douglas K. Morrison, Chicago, IL* [8/21/77]

A: By definition, an "infield fly" does *not* include a bunt attempt. It's not fair to penalize a smart defense for the batter's inability to bunt. And with the Indians, that's a lot of inability.

Out of Left Field

Q: Bases loaded. The batter wallops one which rolls to the center field fence. But his mighty swing goes around and hits the catcher on the side of the head. The catcher falls forward, landing unconscious on top of home plate and completely covering it. Can the runner on third come to the plate and roll the catcher off it so he and his mates can score? Or does the catcher have the plate so completely blocked that the shortstop can run in with the relay and tag all the runners as they try to find the plate? —*Bill Morton, Mansfield, OH* [9/22/90]

A: Never move anyone who has suffered a concussion. Leave that up to the medics. No defensive player is allowed to block a base without possession of the ball. So each runner who came to the plate would be awarded it because of the obstruction. They merely would have to touch the catcher.

NEVER ASSUME

Q: No outs, guy on first. Batter hits a ground ball to the shortstop. He fields it, touches second for the out. His throw pulls the first baseman off the bag. A good throw would have had him but now he's safe at first. I say it's no error. My teammate says it's an error. Who's right? —*Joe Wells, Perrysburg, OH* [7/23/78]

A: You are. It's simply scored as a force out at second. According to the rules of scoring, a double play *never* can be assumed, even when it appears obvious.

CLOSEST TO THE BALL

Q: I enjoy scoring baseball games and this one came up in a recent Indians game. With runners on first and second and one out, the batter lifted a high fly toward third. Brook Jacoby slipped and the ball fell fair. The ump called the batter out because of the infield fly rule and the runners didn't try to advance. Who gets the putout? —*Jeff Welch, Mansfield, OH* [6/2/89]

A: Always give the putout to the fielder you think could have made the catch under ordinary circumstances, which is usually the fielder closest to the ball. In this case, give the putout to Jacoby.

TRIPLE PLAY!

Q: In major league baseball, how is it possible to execute an unassisted triple play? Who else beside Ron Hansen has done it? —*Kim Evangelisti, South Euclid, OH* [1/24/81]

A: Hansen is one of eight. The others were Neal Ball, our own Bill Wamby, George Burns, Ernest Padgett, Glenn Wright, Johnny Cooney, and Johnny Neun. Wamby was a second baseman, Neun and Burns first basemen, and the others were shortstops.

The way it usually went was this: There were runners on first and second in a hit-and-run situation. The batter hit a line drive to the infielder, who tagged second base and then the runner coming to second.

The first baseman did it by catching the line drive, running toward second to tag the runner who had been on first and then tagging second. See, nothing to it.

Out of Left Field

Q: Major league game. Bottom of the ninth, two outs, tied score, runner on third, count on batter is two strikes. The batter swings and misses a pitch in the dirt that bounces up and sticks in the umpire's mask. The batter heads for the dugout as the runner breaks for home and the catcher jumps on top of the umpire and tries to dislodge the ball. The runner crosses home plate as the batter realizes it is an uncaught strike and races to first before he reaches the dugout. The catcher tries to remove the umpire's mask to throw the whole thing, ball and all, to first, but it snags in the umpire's hair. Finally, the catcher grabs the umpire by the arm and they run together to the batter and before the batter reaches first, the catcher takes the umpire's arm and forces him to touch the batter. Is the batter out? Does the run score? Must the catcher force the umpire's face into the batter so the ball touches him? Is it umpire's interference? Please do not use my name as I have a bet riding on this and it's embarrassing. —*Mrs. R. G., Lorain, OH* [10/10/85]

A: Your question conjures up all sorts of hilarious images. I can picture the catcher pulling at the umpire, then dragging him toward first base. I'd pay to see that. But the rules eliminate all that silly fun. When the pitch lodges in the umpire's mask, the ball is dead immediately. All runners advance one base and on strike three the batter goes to first base. Game over. Enshrine the mask and the ball in the Hall of Fame.

GOLDEN GLOVE

Q: In a game, my third baseman threw his glove at the ball in foul territory. He didn't think he'd be able to reach it in time and he was afraid it would roll fair. The umpire gave the batter three bases because he threw his glove at the ball. I protested on the grounds there is no penalty for throwing your glove at a foul ball. Who's right, me or the ump? —*Ken P. Wohlgemuth, Euclid* [8/10/69]

A: You are. The batter gets at least three bases if a thrown glove *hits a fair ball*. There is no penalty if the glove misses the ball. Nor is there a penalty for hitting a *foul* ball with your glove.

Your man made an intelligent play and was penalized by an ignorant umpire.

·················· **CENTERFIELD THRILLS** ··················

Q: Two outs. Batter hits a high, deep drive to center. The center fielder bobbles the ball for a while. Meanwhile the batter makes it home before the outfielder finally manages to hold the ball. Does the run count? —*Bil Graper, Madison, OH* [8/10/89]

A: No, this is a legal catch. Inning over. The center fielder merely gave everyone a thrill.

·················· **BOBBLING THE BALL** ··················

Q: Let's say the Indians are playing the Tigers. Kirk Gibson is up with a man on third and one out. He hits a long fly to Brett Butler. The runner on third is getting ready to tag up. Butler catches the ball but bobbles it. Can he keep on tapping it around until he gets so close that the man on third can't tag up and score? —*John Marchuk, Lorain, OH* [7/11/85]

A: No. The instant Butler touches the ball, the runner can go. Otherwise, you'd see better juggling acts than in a circus.

·················· **FAN INTERFERENCE** ··················

Q: In the Cleveland-Milwaukee game, April 12, Charlie Spikes was called out because a fan interfered with the catcher. Why penalize the batter for what some fan did? What's to stop the home fans from interfering every time the ball is hit near the stands and thus getting the batter called out? —*Carlton Staeding* [4/20/75]

A: You ask why penalize the batter? Why penalize the fielder? If a ball is playable he should be allowed to try to catch it without any interference. You suggest that the home fan purposely can try to help his team by such interference. So could a visiting fan. Who's to say what the fan's allegiance is? Should the umpire check out his driver's license or give him a lie-detector test?

The rule is a good one. I thought the umpire was right in making the call he did in Milwaukee. That ball could have been caught if the fans hadn't interfered.

But after making the call, I would have had the fan ejected from the park. Fans are there to watch the game, not play it.

Out of Left Field

Q: Regulation Little League game. Bases loaded, bottom of the last inning. Two outs, score is tied. The batter walks. Instead of going to first base, the batter jumps up and down and yells, "Whoopie," and runs off the field, never touching first base. The pitcher, after getting the ball back, throws to first base. The fielding team has not left the field. Does the game go into extra innings, or does it end? *—Bill Blackwood, Norwalk, OH* [7/22/75]

A: Since the Little League rules are similar to the major league rules—the official baseball rules—the batter is out for running off the field without touching first base, since an appeal was made on him. An experienced umpire will say to the batter, "Be sure to tag first base," but the ump doesn't have to. It's the batter's responsibility. *All* bases must be tagged in baseball, unless the crazy high school rules are used.

The batter yelled, "Whoopie," too soon.

FAIR OR FOUL?

Q: Would you please give me a ruling on the following play: The batter hits a ball down the third-base line. The ball hits about a foot in fair territory two-thirds of the way to the bag. It is hooking and comes up over the bag in the air. Before the ball hits the ground again the third baseman, who is behind the bag, reaches into foul territory and fields the ball. Is it fair or foul? I've always believed that unless the ball hits the bag or behind it in fair territory, it is a foul ball. The ump called it fair. I disagreed, but you know how that is. Of the registered umps we have asked, they are split about 50-50. Same way with the guys at work. We need your help. *—David O. Auble, Fostoria, OH* [9/20/80]

A: It is absolutely and positively a fair ball. Those fellows who said otherwise don't know fair from foul.

UNSPORTSMANLIKE CONDUCT

Q: In a men's slow-pitch softball tourney, I was playing short. With a man on first and no outs, a high pop was hit behind second base. As I called for it I saw the guy who hit it stand in frustration, rather than run to first base. So I acted like I would catch it, but I dropped it purposely to start a double play. The other team was upset and yelled obscenities at me but I didn't care. If a guy doesn't run he deserves to be out. Isn't this play legal according to the rules? —*Matt Lissy, Mansfield, OH* [10/11/90]

A: If the ball hits your glove and then you purposely drop it—as you apparently did—the ball is dead and the batter is automatically out. The runner must return to first base. No double play. If you had allowed the ball to hit the ground *untouched* and then taken your chances on a double play, you would have done it properly. Batters should run everything out. On the other hand, fielders shouldn't be allowed to catch balls and then drop them on purpose. This freezes base runners and is considered unsportsmanlike.

·················· **FIELDER'S CHOICE** ··················

Q: Runner on first. Batter hits ground ball to shortstop. A play is made on the runner at second base, but he beats the throw and no play is made at first. How would the play be scored? Same play, but shortstop momentarily bobbles the ground ball. How would it be scored? In both plays, if the shortstop had thrown directly to first the batter would have been out. —*Jim Lange, Cleveland, OH,* [8/19/79]

A: In the first instance, it's a fielder's choice. The batter is charged with a time at bat. No hit. In the second case, give the shortstop an error and the batter a time at bat.

Scorers always should use pencils with erasers.

··············· **UNASSISTED TRIPLE PLAY!** ···············

Q: My mother was telling us about a triple play she saw at the Stadium. I would like to know what teams and players were involved and what positions they played. I know it occurred after 1948. —*Ann Marnie, Willowick, OH* [6/1/75]

A: There were several triple plays since that date at the Stadium but only *one unassisted* triple play so I am assuming this is the one your mother remembers. It occurred July 30, 1968, against the Washington Senators and the Indians were on the wrong end. In the first inning the Indians had Dave Nelson on second and Russ Snyder on first and there were no outs, of course. The batter was Joe Azcue. With the count 3-2, the run-and-hit was flashed. Azcue lined to Ron Hansen, playing short for the Senators. He tagged second, doubling Nelson, and then he tagged Snyder who was coming toward him.

Nothing to it when everybody cooperates.

INSECURE POSSESSION

Q: Me and my friend are having an argument about this play: A fielder is running in for a sinking line drive. The ball hits his glove and knocks it off his hand, but the ball stays in the glove. Is the batter safe or out? Will you please hurry up? —*Andrew (Sharpy) Froehlich* [8/21/59]

A: Sorry we couldn't hurry, Sharpy, but we're swamped with questions and we try to answer them in the order received. The batter is safe, because the player must have "secure possession" of the ball in order to make a legal catch. In this case, the glove made the catch, the player didn't.

THAT BALL IS ALIVE

Q: A runner is on first, nobody out and the count on the batter is one-and-one. On the next pitch the runner takes off and steals second. However, the batter foul-tipped the ball and the catcher hung on. Does the batter have to go back to first or is this a live ball. We couldn't find the rule. —*Ron Rodriguez* [8/31/75]

A: When a foul tip goes "sharp and direct" into the catcher's glove and is caught by him it's the same as a missed strike. The ball is live and the runner can steal at his own peril. In your case the runner is safe at second. But if the catcher drops the ball, it becomes dead and the runner would have to return. This should tell a smart catcher to drop the ball if he sees he has no chance to get the runner.

·················· INFIELD FLY TROUBLE ··················

Q: Regarding the infield fly rule do the runners have to be tagged out after attempting to advance after the infield fly has been called? It seems to me that once the batter is automatically out the force play does not exist. —*Sara E. Keller* [6/26/77]

A: Since the batter is out the runners do not have to advance. Therefore, there can't be a force play on an infield fly. The runners must be tagged if they try to advance. Of course, they can't leave before the ball is caught. If they do they can be called out on appeals after the catch.

The infield fly rule sometimes causes awfully sticky situations. This corner long has suggested one change in the rule. The infield fly must be caught. If it isn't, the batter should be awarded first base. This would eliminate all the confusing incidents. Moreover, why should a batter be out if the ball isn't caught? But nobody listens to me.

·················· FORCE FIELD ··················

Q: Bases are loaded, one out. Batter hits to the pitcher, who throws home. If the catcher then throws to third is it a force if the base is tagged, or must the runner be touched? —*H.R.* [5/24/77]

A: Tag the base. It's a force.

But the play rarely is made that way. Usually the catcher throws to first base to complete the double play. Reason: It takes much longer for the batter to get to first after his swing than it does for a runner to advance from second to third. Unless, of course, the runner is pulling a truck.

·················· THE TOP OF THE FENCE ··················

Q: Would you please give your opinion on this play? Our playing field is fenced in with a three-foot-high high chain link fence. The opposing team has the bases loaded and the batter hits a long fly to center. It is sinking and lands on the top rail of the fence and bounces up into the air. The center fielder reaches over the fence and catches the ball. He throws it back into the infield where time is eventually called with runners on second

and third. The umpires, after consulting the local playing rules, call it a home run because this example is given: "If a ball is hit over the fence it is a home run." My personal feelings are that it is not a home run since it didn't go over the fence on the fly.
—*James A. Shell, Newark, OH* [7/25/77]

A: Here's a case where you can throw away the rules book. According to the book the ball must go over *in flight* to be a homer, which means it must go over without touching any obstacle except a player. Certainly the fence is an obstacle.

But the rulemakers say they didn't quite intend this to be the case when the ball hits the top of the fence. I checked with members of the rules committee. They say that the top of the fence is considered the boundary. If the ball hits the top and goes to the other side, it's a homer. If it comes back toward the playing field, it isn't.

Specifically, if a ball hits the top of the fence and bounces back against a player and then bounces over, it's a two-base hit. If it bounces back and is caught, it remains in play. If it is caught on the other side of the boundary after hitting the top of the fence, it's a homer.

Therefore, in your case it's a homer.

It think it should be, by rule, a ground-rule double but the boys who wrote the books say they didn't mean what they wrote. Go fight them.

·············· **Out of Left Field** ··················

Q: This play occurred in a slow-pitch game in an A.S.A. league: Runner on first base. Batter fouls first pitch to deep left, out of play. A spectator retrieved the ball and tossed it to the left fielder, who was already in position for the next pitch and when the next pitch was delivered, he was holding the ball previously fouled. The batter lined a single to the left. The left fielder tossed the "dead" ball aside, in fair territory, and fielded the base hit cleanly.

The runner from first, running with head down, hit second and saw the "dead" ball rolling free in left center and continued full-speed toward third. He was easy prey for the short throw and was ruled out. Should the play be allowed to stand?
—*James Hamro, Parma, OH* [9/30/75]

A: This is a dandy and it's not covered specifically in the rules book. Which means it *is* covered specifically by Rule 10—Power and Duties of an umpire. This rule gives him the authority to make decisions on plays not specifically covered by the rules.

In this case it would be unfair to declare the runner out. Put him back at second base where he normally would have stopped on that single.

If anybody wants to argue with this call—don't. Tom Mason, the national official interpreter for the Amateur Softball Association, agrees. It's the only fair thing to do. And that's what umpires are supposed to be—fair. Fair enough?

·················· HOW MANY APPEALS? ·····················

Q: None out, runners on first and second. Batter triples. The third baseman calls for the ball, claiming the runner from second missed third. Losing this appeal, he claimed the runner from first missed third. The umpire ruled his first appeal counted as a play and, therefore, the second appeal came too late and could not be recognized. Correct? —*Lloyd Realty, Tiffin, OH* [4/11/85]

A: No. It is legal to appeal at every base on all runners. One appeal doesn't close the door. It is the responsibility of *all* runners to touch *all* bases. Of course, the rules also prevent anyone from making a travesty of the game, so if appeals are constantly being made without foundation, the umpire can say "enough." But in your case, the ump was totally wrong.

·················· A FOURTH OUT ·····················

Q: I was involved in this situation in college. Runner on second and third, one out. The batter flies deep to left. The runners tag and try to advance. The left fielder throws to third because he knows he can't get the runner at the plate. The runner from second is tagged out at third. The team in the field appeals that the runner from third left too soon and the umpire calls him out. I have heard of a "fourth out," but I'm not sure. What's the correct ruling and who gets credit for the extra out if this is the case? —*Steve Tomnie, Lorain, OH* [7/6/89]

7

Seventh-Inning Stretch

Historical Questions

Q: Perhaps you can provide the answer to a question recently
put to me: What is the origin of the seventh-inning stretch?
—*Harry W. Wise, Kirtland, OH* [11/16/02]

A: This is another one of those questions that's asked at least
once a year. It is popularly believed that the custom goes back
to 1910, when President William Howard Taft, while attend-
ing a game in Pittsburgh, found his bulk a little too much for
his seat, stood up and stretched in the seventh inning. The
crowd, thinking he was about the leave, stood up in respect for
the chief executive, thus starting the custom. But the truth is
that way back in 1869, according to a letter written by Harry
Wright, captain for the Cincinnati Red Stockings, "The specta-
tors all arise between halves of the seventh inning, extend their
arms and legs and sometimes walk about. In doing so, they
enjoy the relief afforded by relaxation from the long posture
upon hard benches."

The seats haven't become much softer in 133 years. In summary, the fans got up in the middle of the seventh since the
days baseball was in its infancy because they couldn't stand
sitting any longer.

ORIGIN OF THE INDIANS

Q: What was the Cleveland baseball team nicknamed before it became the Indians and how did it become to be named the Indians? —*Bob George, Lyndhurst, OH* [5/27/89]

A: Cleveland had its first professional team in 1869, the league was the National Association, and it was known as the Forest Citys, for Cleveland then was a city of trees and nicknamed "Forest City." In 1889, now a member of the National League, the team became the Spiders, supposedly because so many of its players were tall and skinny.

In 1900, Cleveland joined a new league, which was to become the American League the following year. The new club was called the Blues or Bluebirds, because of its blue uniforms. The players wanted a tougher name, so they voted to call themselves the Broncos in 1902. The next year fans were asked to select a new name through a newspaper contest, and the team became the Naps, in honor of Napoleon (Larry) Lajoie, the popular second baseman. After the 1914 season, Lajoie, his career waning at 40, was released and picked up by the Philadelphia Athletics.

Another name, therefore, became necessary. Again, a newspaper contest was held. A longtime fan wrote a letter suggesting the team be called the Indians, in honor of Louis Francis Sockalexis, who had played for the Spiders in 1897-99, the first Indian ever to play major-league ball. The suggestions caught on and the team has been the Indians ever since.

Actually Sockalexis, an outfielder, had only one good year. He batted .338 in 1897 and was a sub the following two seasons. But in that one year he clearly made a strong impression. According to accounts, Sockalexis was partial to "firewater," which hastened his departure from the majors.

The Chief, as he was known, became a ball player against his father's wishes. His father, the actual chief of the Penobscot tribe in Old Town, Maine, hated baseball, calling it "a game children played with sticks and balls." After his son got a scholarship to Holy Cross College to play baseball, the old Chief was so upset he decided to go to the Great White Father in Washington, President Grover Cleveland, and ask him to prevent his son from this foolishness.

The chief built a birch-bark canoe, paddled across the Penobscot River to the Atlantic Ocean and finally to the Potomac. When he got to Washington he discovered the president was away. For months and months the chief kept paddling to catch up to the president, but always seemed to just miss him.

Finally, a Washington paper learned of the Chief's search, published the story and Maine congressmen obtained a meeting between the two "chiefs." President Cleveland was sympathetic to the elder Sockalexis, but said he didn't have the authority to stop the son from playing ball.

By the time the old Chief got back to Maine, Louis already was at Holy Cross, starring in football as well as baseball. Afterward he was signed by the Spiders.

Louis now is in the Holy Cross Hall of Fame. He died just three years after his father. On the reservation in Maine is a monument in his honor. A bronze plaque with crossed bats reads, "In memory of Louis Sockalexis, whose athletic achievements while at Holy Cross College and later with the Cleveland baseball team won for him national fame. Born October 24, 1871, died December 24, 1913."

In back of the monument is a wooden marker in the shape of a diamond. It reads, "This is the grave of the famous Louis Sockalexis who was the first Indian to become a major league baseball player. He joined the Cleveland team . . . He was a talented and spectacular player and colorful in all his actions. Soon after the Cleveland team was renamed the Cleveland Indians, the name it still carries today."

·············· **HOW LONG BEHIND THE PLATE?** ··············

Q: How many years has the umpire been calling 'em from behind the plate?" —*Frank Packard, Cleveland, OH* [5/14/59]

A: History fails to single out the first brave man who did so. In the early days (1860), the umpire stood on the sidelines. The batter would ask the pitcher for a ball in a certain area, high or low. The umpire would judge it a ball or strike, according

to how close he came to the batter's request. Nine balls consti-
tuted a walk. The umpire also had the privilege of consulting
with the fans and other players before rendering his decision.
Later, a specific strike zone was established, and in 1882, the
rules insisted the umpire make his own decisions without
assistance. As far as we can determine, just about this time,
the umpire moved as close as possible to home plate to see the
pitches more clearly. He would walk to the ball park in his blue
suit, take his cap out of his pocket, step behind the plate and
call, "Play ball." There was only one umpire per game and he
moved behind the pitcher's mound and called the pitches from
there when there was a runner on base. The umpire used no
chest protector behind the plate and the "bird cage" or mask
was shunned by many of them at the beginning. According to
A. G. Spalding's 1895 baseball guide, "several umpires have
been killed outright while occupying this dangerous position."
In comparison, today's umpires—four per game—have rock-
ing-chair jobs.

·················· **THE BABE'S LOST HOMERS** ··················

Q: I seem to recall that Babe Ruth would have had more home
runs in his career, but there was a period of time when a
baseball that passed the fair side of the foul ball but landed
in the stands on the foul side was called a foul ball. No one I
have discussed this with ever heard of this rule. Fact or fiction?
—*Bob Potts, Lorain, OH* [4/10/98]

A: Fact. Prior to 1920 the ball was judged fair or foul according to
where it landed, not where it passed the pole. So if a batted ball
was fair as it crossed the foul pole but curved around it and
landed foul it was a foul ball. Ruth entered the majors in 1914
as a pitcher. He continued to pitch exclusively until 1918 and,
by then, had hit 10 homers. In 1918 and 1919 he pitched and
played the outfield and in those two years hit 40 homers. Thus,
he had a total of 50 homers before the rule was changed. The
late John Tattersall, a baseball historian who researched all
of the Babe's homers, found that he lost none because of that
"foul" rule. An equally interesting rule, relative to the home
run, was the one that gave a batter a homer if his hit bounced

into the stands or over the fence, providing the barrier was at
least 250 feet from the plate. In 1931 these bouncing balls were
changed to ground-rule doubles. But Babe never got one of
those cheapies. Every Ruth clout was into the seats or over the
fence.

·················· **Out of Left Field** ··················

Q: A friend who formerly lived in Cleveland claims the city generally has a curse on it and the Indians specifically. He claims
the Indians were cursed by Bobby Bragan after he was fired
as manager in 1958. He says there was an exorcism at second
base a few years ago to remove it. Is there anything to the
Bobby Bragan story? *—Paul Livingston, Mansfield, OH* [9/9/89]

A: The Bragan myth is exactly that, pure baloney. It was con-
cocted by a radio talk show host and the station, as a stunt,
staged an exorcism at second base. Bragan managed the Indians briefly in 1958. The general manager, Frank Lane, got rid
of him almost as quickly as he did many of the players. Maybe
Lane was the jinx. The best exorcism would be a lineup of better ball players.

·············· **THE BABE AT THE STADIUM** ··············

Q: My friend says Babe Ruth played at Cleveland Stadium. I say
he never did. Who's right? *—Tim Hinkel, Mentor, OH* [6/30/90]

A: Your friend. The Babe played several games at the Stadium in
1933. He was a member of the Yankees then, and the Indians
played all their games at the Stadium that season. But the
Babe never hit a home run there.

·············· **FELLER'S SENSATIONAL DEBUT** ··············

Q: Before Bob Feller became a regular member of the Indians he
pitched in an exhibition game against the St. Louis Cardinals
when they had the famous Gas House Gang of Pepper Martin,
Leo Durocher, the Dean brothers, and other notables. I think
the game was played at League Park. How did Feller do?
—Charles Richter, Chardon, OH [9/29/90]

A: Bob was brought to Cleveland in June of 1936 at age 17, just

after his high school semester was over. He had been scheduled to report to a minor league club. Instead, it was decided to
let him pitch for the Rosenblums, a Class A sandlot team here.
In those days a local Class A sandlot club was equivalent to a
middle division minor league team. Meanwhile, he worked out
at League Park. The Indians had an exhibition game scheduled
against the Cardinals for July 6 and by pitching Feller, the
Tribe management thought the game would draw more fans,
as well as be a test for the schoolboy. He pitched the fourth,
fifth, and sixth innings, allowed one hit and an unearned run
and fanned eight. A crowd of 10,000 attended the weekday
exhibition. After that the Indians immediately put him on the
big league roster and he became the talk of the town.

EARLY EXITS

Q: When Mike Hargrove, the Indians' manager, was thrown out
in the first inning of the second playoff game against the Red
Sox and then Dwight Gooden, the Indians' pitcher, was thrown
out a few pitches later, it raised this question among some of
us. What is the shortest time a manager has been in a game
before getting thrown out? Also, what is the shortest time for a
pitcher? *—Mrs. Josephine Drissman, North Madison, OH* [10/19/98]

A: No records are kept on this. But there have been several
instances in which the manager was thrown out before the
first pitch. The umpire and the manager continued an argument from the day before and the umpire preferred peace
and pointed his thumb to the showers. If memory serves, Earl
Weaver, the fiery former Baltimore Orioles manager, once
was ejected when he was giving the umps his lineup card with
a few choice words. The most celebrated early ejection of a
pitcher—and probably the earliest—came on June 23, 1917,
in Fenway Park, with the Red Sox playing the Washington
Senators. Babe Ruth was pitching for the Sox. The game was
less than three minutes old when plate umpire Brick Owens
threw him out. Ruth didn't like Owens' calls on the first batter, Ray Morgan, who walked, and he began berating Owens.
According to accounts, the ump said, "Get in there and pitch
or you'll be out of there in one minute." Ruth replied, "If I'm

out of there, you'll get a punch in the jaw." Owens didn't wait the minute and told Ruth he was gone. Ruth did take a swing at the ump, but fortunately missed his jaw. Ruth was gone, of course, having lasted only a fraction over three minutes and just those few pitches. Gooden threw at least 20 pitches. More than incidentally, Ruth's replacement, Ernie Shore, is now in the record books. The batter Ruth put on, Morgan, was thrown out stealing almost immediately and Shore retired the next 26 batters in order and was credited with a perfect game.

SOME CONTACT HITTER

Q: While I was listening to a ballgame this summer, Ralph Kiner, who broadcasts Mets games, said that Joe DiMaggio struck out only 13 times in one season. Is this true and is it a record?
—*J. A., New Haven, CT* [11/14/98]

A: It is true that Joe DiMaggio fanned only 13 times in 1941. But it's no record. Joe Sewell, a Cleveland Indians shortstop, holds the distinction for striking out the fewest times. In 1925 he fanned only four times in 155 games. And to prove it was no fluke he did it again in 1929. Sewell came up to the majors in 1920 when the Indians' shortstop, Ray Chapman, was killed by a pitched ball. He helped the Indians win the World Series that year and remained 14 seasons in the big leagues, the last few with the Yankees. He struck out only 114 times in 7,132 at-bats. No wonder he is in the Hall of Fame.

TICKET PRICES

Q: I wonder if you could tell me the price of general admission and grandstand seat at League Park during the Indians' 1920 championship season? —*Frank Cox, Mansfield, OH* [11/25/89]

A: According to an Indians' ad at the time grandstand tickets were $1, pavilion (general admission) 75 cents, and bleacher seats were 50 cents. The grandstand seat was the best in the house. I recall sitting right behind home plate for a buck. This was around 1930, Depression time. My mother had a fit when she heard I spent a dollar to see a ballgame.

SILLY SACRIFICE

Q: Please tell my why, in a baseball game, a batter gets credit for a sacrifice fly when he swings for the fences with a runner on third and fewer than two outs and the runner scores. I always figured a sacrifice meant what the word implies—giving up a chance to go for a hit in order to advance a runner. I got sick of these announcers giving these prima donna fence-busters credit for a sacrifice when really they don't deserve it. It just keeps their batting averages above .200. —*Richard C. Volz, Sandusky, OH* [11/16/89]

A: You are not alone in questioning the validity of the sacrifice fly scoring rule. This controversy has been going on since the rule first was put into the books in 1907. At that time those who argued that a batter whose fly scores a run should get a sacrifice, because that's what he basically was trying to do, had their way. Those who disagreed said, "If you're going to be that silly, why not be consistently silly and give the batter a sacrifice every time his fly advances a runner? Why just limit it to a fly that scores a run?" So, in 1926, all fly balls that advanced a runner became sacrifices and no official at-bat. Of course, that really was ridiculous and made the point for the anti-sacrifice faction. By 1931 the entire sacrifice fly rule was stricken from the books. But those in favor wouldn't quit, and in 1939 the scoring rules committee returned the sacrifice fly (that scores a run) to the book. Now the other side raised a holler and, in 1940, it was stricken again. It remained out of the book until 1954. Then the pro-sacrifice folks on the committee were in the majority and put it back in the book. It's been there ever since. Those who are with you have not been able to muster enough votes to kill it and they have virtually given up. I think it's now a permanent part of the game, and I'm afraid you're just going to have to suffer. But the above history should give you some consolation. You are not alone. I think it's a nutty rule, too, put in just to raise batting averages.

AN ATHLETIC ELEPHANT

Q: How did it come about that Connie Mack's American League team was called the Athletics and what was the significance

of the elephant as the team's logo? —*Carl J. Keller, Norwalk, OH*
[7/1/89]

A: The name Athletics was a popular one in Philadelphia before
the American League was born in 1901. Several sports teams in
the area had used it in the latter part of the 19th century. Also,
when Mack was offered the Philadelphia franchise in the new
league he was advised to get together with Benjamin Shibe,
owner of A. J. Reach Sporting Goods Company, as his money
man. Shibe had backed teams in the American Association and
Eastern League and they, too, had been known as the Athletics. So it was a natural for Mack and Shibe to agree their new
Philadelphia club would be called the Athletics. As the team
was being assembled, John McGraw, a star of that era and the
player-manager of Baltimore in the infant American League,
scoffed at Mack's talent and said, "They'll be the white elephant of the league." Instead of being offended by the remark,
Mack decided to use it to his advantage. He immediately made
the symbol of his team a white elephant. Mack's team soon
became a power in the new league, but by then McGraw had
moved to the National League as manager of the New York
Giants. Both Mack and McGraw are in the Hall of Fame today.
And the Philadelphia franchise is now in Oakland, where the
team is still known as the Athletics and its symbol is the white
elephant.

·· **Out of Left Field** ·······················

Q: Why wasn't there a World Series in 1904? —*Joseph Hanick,
Marion, OH* [9/10/88]

A: There wasn't one in 1901 and 1902 either. The American
League was established in 1901 and the veteran National
League refused to recognize it. There had been open warfare
between them. The American League often attempted to
raid the older loop of some of its stars. But in 1903, when
the Boston Red Sox and the Pittsburg Pirates won their
respective pennants, the owners of these two teams decided
to cool things by playing a best-of-nine series for the "world
championship," although there was nothing official about this
series. The upstart American League won in eight games. The

following season the Red Sox won the pennant again but the National League champs, the New York Giants, wouldn't play them. The Giants' owner, John T. Brush, and manager, John McGraw, were still too angry at the American League. So there was no postseason meeting between the two loops. There was a considerable outcry from the fans, many of whom called the Giants "chicken." It wasn't that the Giants were scared. Their management simply continued to look at the young league with disdain and said, "We're the only real major league champions." The following year, 1905, the Giants won out in their league again, while the Philadelphia Phillies triumphed in the American League. This time Brush, the Giants' owner, magnanimously bowed to public opinion and agreed to a play-off. In fact, he set up the guidelines for what was to become the annual "fall classic," a revenue formula and a best-of-seven format. The Giants, with Christy Mathewson and "Iron Man" Joe McGinnity pitching all but one inning of the entire series for the Giants, beat the Athletics in five games. I mention this only because some pitchers now complain if they have to pitch more than seven innings every fifth day. Mathewson pitched 27 innings within six days and shut out the Athletics in all three games.

·················· **MOUND MATTERS** ··················

Q: Can you write something on the elevation of the pitcher's mound? When was its inception? Why was it necessary, etc.?
   —Al F. Trizzino, Mayfield Heights, OH [7/7/88]

A: Not even the library at the Cooperstown Hall of Fame, the best baseball library in the world, has complete documentation on the evolution of the pitcher's mound. Nothing about a mound was mentioned in the rules book until 1903. But photos of the games in the 1800s show the fields slanting upward from the plate to the mound. In other words, the pitchers always threw downhill. Hitters apparently liked this, for it gave them a better view of the release of the ball, so they didn't complain. Pitchers, too, preferred pitching downhill.

In any event, not until 1893 did the rules even make a pitcher's rubber mandatory. It was a rubber slab, one foot long by four inches deep and for the first time the precise distance of the pitcher's rubber from the plate was specified at 60 feet 6 inches, the same as it is today. Before that, pitchers were closer to the batter. The rubber was placed on a small mound, although the book said nothing about one. Two years later, the pitcher's rubber was extended another foot and the depth increased two inches.

Because the groundskeepers began to play around with the mound to satisfy their pitchers, some of the hills grew to small mountains, so in 1903 the rulemakers finally wrote "mound" into the book and specified that it could not be more than 15 inches above the infield level. This still allowed groundskeepers to play around with it, since no minimum was established and some of the groundskeepers—Emil Bossard, the genius at League Park, and the Stadium—custom-built the mound each day for the Indians' pitcher. Some liked it high, some lower.

Rival pitchers—and hitters—screamed about the constant changes in the mound, so in 1969 the rules established that the top of the mound "shall be 10 inches above home plate." Also, the slope toward the foul lines is clearly spelled out. The majors send out supervisors to the various parks to check the dimensions. They come in without notice and teams who are found to have mounds not in compliance with the rules are heavily fined and must correct them immediately.

························· **WHY BAT LAST?** ·························

Q: I've been doing some research about baseball back in 1902 and I've discovered something. On every day's box scores for that period I find at least one game where the home team was listed as batting the top half of every inning. Was there a rule giving the home team an option of batting first at the turn of the century? —*Timothy Wayne, Lorain, OH* [1/21/88]

A: This will come as a surprise to many longtime baseball fans. Until 1950, the captain of the home team had the option of having his club bat first or last. Initially the home captain occasionally did choose to bat first, but soon teams realized it was to the advantage to have the last crack at winning. So as major league baseball progressed after the turn of the century, it became automatic for the home club to decide to bat last. As a consequence, when the rules book was rectified in 1950 it became mandatory for the home club to bat last. The captain no longer had a choice.

·············· **IMPERFECT PERFECTION** ··············

Q: Several weeks ago you carried a question about a perfect game in baseball. I always thought it was one in which the pitcher faced only 27 batters and they all were retired. Yet there is a record of Babe Ruth, when he was a pitcher, walking the first man he faced. Then he got thrown out of the game by the umpire. The pitcher, who came in to relieve him, while pitching to the second batter, had the runner thrown out trying to steal second. He then retired all the following batters in order and was credited with a perfect no-hit game. How come? He faced only 26 men. —*Robert E. Roberts, Lorain, OH* [12/13/84]

A: What you described occurred June 23, 1917. Ruth, pitching for the Red Sox, walked leadoff hitter Ray Morgan, then began to abuse plate umpire Brick Owens. Owens ordered Ruth to pitch within one minute or, "You'll be out of there." Ruth replied, "If I'm out, you'll get a punch in the jaw." Owens immediately threw Ruth out. Ruth rushed the ump, swung, hit him on the left ear and the police hurried onto the field and Ruth was quickly removed. Ernie Shore, sitting on the bench, was called to the mound by Manager Jack Barry. He was allowed the customary five pitches before facing the second batter. Morgan tried to steal second, was thrown out, and Shore retired the remaining 26 Washington batters with relative ease. The Records Committee decided to include Shore's brilliant effort on the Perfect Game list, with an asterisk, explaining how it was done. There are many who maintain his name should be scratched, for if a pitcher repeated Shore's performance, under the present rule, he couldn't be credited with a perfect game. The rule now—not in effect during Shore's time—is this: a pitcher can't be credited with a shutout unless he pitches a complete game. If Shore didn't pitch a complete game and, hence, not a shutout, how could he have pitched a perfect game? In any case, he's on the Perfect Game list now, plus asterisk, and your question provided the opportunity to relate a unique page from baseball's engrossing history.

WHY A CAP?

Q: Recently I was asked why major league players had to wear baseball caps while playing. I did not have an answer but was told it was a league rule. Will you please explain the reason for this rule? —*Miro G. Horvath, Euclid, OH* [7/25/77]

A: Baseball originally was a game played under the sun and a cap with a peak was essential. Even under lights it helps. Almost from the very beginning it became part of the official equipment. Besides it looks better than bushy hair.

And balding players love it.

A RECORD TAG

Q: I have been thinking about this since Mark McGwire hit his 62nd home run. He rounded first and missed the base, but came back to touch it, then he continued around the bases. What would have been the result if he hadn't touched first but continued around the bases and tagged home? —*Herb Hart, Mansfield, OH* [9/9/98]

A: If the defensive team had properly appealed his failure to tag first, McGwire would have been out and wouldn't have been credited with 62. Since the Cardinals were playing the Cubs, a team fighting for the wild card, I doubt if the Cubs would have looked the other way and refused to appeal. But since Mac did tag the bag, we'll never know.

THE CURSE OF AL ROSEN?

Q: I put this question to several baseball fans and none knew the answer. What baseball player was involved in two World Series 35 years apart and losing each one in four straight games? —*Frank Durkalski, Chester Township, OH* [11/4/89]

A: It's obvious you know and that you're testing me. You're thinking of Al Rosen. He was the Indians' slugging third baseman when they won the pennant in 1954 by setting an all-time American League record of 111 victories. Then, they lost the

Worlds Series to the New York Giants in four straight when a pinchhitter named Dusty Rhodes got some home runs just inside the foul line 257 feet from home plate in the odd-shaped Polo Grounds.

The Indians' Vic Wertz hit one to dead center with two men on that would have been a homer in any other park. But center was so deep in the Polo Grounds, Willie Mays finally caught up with ball, his back to the infield, about 480 feet from the plate. Rosen, in fact, was one of the runners on base at the time.

The same Al Rosen is now general manager of the San Francisco Giants, who just lost in four straight to the Oakland Athletics. These are the same Giants who moved to the Bay from New York. Rosen must be wondering if he isn't a jinx. But at least when he's around, teams reach the World Series. The Indians haven't won anything since he's been gone.

················· **FIRST GAME UNDER LIGHTS** ················

Q: Could you tell me when was the first night baseball game— played under lights, of course? —*Howard Burkhardt, Lorain, OH* [6/21/89]

A: The first major league night game was played in Crosley Field, Cincinnati, May 25, 1935. The Reds beat the Phillies, 2-1. But night baseball was played long before this. In the late 1920s the Kansas City Monarchs, of the old Negro League and starring pitcher, Satchel Paige, carried portable lights on their barnstorming tours and hoisted them night after night as they moved from town to town.

And history records that in September 1880 two amateur baseball teams met at Nantasket Beach, Mass. and played a complete nine-inning game under arc lights strung across the field. The game went smoothly, being completed in 1½ hours. The next recorded night game was played June 2, 1883, in Ft. Wayne, Mich. and there were many night contests after that.

················· Out of Left Field ················

Q: Did Bob Feller ever hit a foul ball into the stands, striking his mother? —*Dan Weber, Euclid, OH* [7/13/89]

A: He didn't hit the ball, but he threw the pitch. It happened on

Mother's Day in Comiskey Park during Feller's third season with the Indians. His mother, father, and sister had come up from Van Meter, Iowa to watch him pitch against the White Sox. They were sitting in the grandstand seats between home and the first base. Marvin Owen was the batter. After several harmless fouls, Owen fouled one that hit Mrs. Feller flush in the face. Bob's follow-through gave him a full view of the sickening sight.

His recollections: "I felt sick, but saw she was conscious. I saw them leading my mother out and my impulse was to run to the stands. I was told the injury was painful but not serious so I kept on pitching. I felt giddy and became wild. I know the Sox scored three runs and I'm not sure how.

"There wasn't anything I could do, so I went on and finished the game and we won. Then I hurried to the hospital. My mother's face was bruised and swollen and she said she had a headache. But she kept smiling and saying, 'I'm all right and don't you go blaming yourself. It wasn't your fault.' That's how she always was.

"She never complained and always encouraged me. Even though I believe she originally would have preferred I didn't play ball. If she had her druthers, she would have been happier, I think, if I had gone on to college or continued to play the trumpet the way I did in the Van Meter Methodist Church."

· · · · · · · · · · · · · · · · · THE STREAK ENDS HERE · · · · · · · · · · · · · · · · ·

Q: When Joe DiMaggio's consecutive game hitting streak was stopped at 56 games, was this game played at League Park or Municipal Stadium and what was the year? —*Kenneth R. Ertle, Massillon, OH* [7/10/77]

A: The date was July 16, 1941, and 67,468 saw the game. League Park couldn't accommodate half that amount.

Yes, it was at the Stadium.

· · · · · · · · · · · · · · · · · LEAGUE PARK LORE · · · · · · · · · · · · · · · · ·

Q: When was League Park built? Where was it located? When did the Indians move from it to Municipal Stadium? —*Bob Moncier, Cleveland, OH* [7/18/76]

A: The first game was played there by the Cleveland Spiders, May 1, 1891. The Spiders were in the National League at that time. The site was chosen by the team's owner, Frank De Haas Robinson. He owned the Payne Avenue and Superior Avenue streetcar lines so he put the ballpark at E. 66th Street and Lexington, which was convenient to both lines. When Cleveland went into the American League in 1901 the same park was used. It was rebuilt in 1910, with new grandstands, etc. and it never was changed much after that.

The Indians played a few games at the Stadium in 1932, and played their full home schedule there in 1933. But the crowds were small and the cost high, so they moved back to League Park and stayed there—except for numerous visits to the Stadium for big games—until the end of the 1946 season. From 1947 on, all their home games have been played at the Stadium.

If you ever get to the East Side, drive past E. 66th and Lexington. You'll see remnants of old League Park. For old fans, it's a trip to nostalgia.

···················· **THE BIGGEST CROWD** ····················

Q: What was the largest attendance for any sporting event held at the Stadium? I would say the 86,000-87,000 during a 1948 World Series game. The person who disagrees says there were more during the Pan-American Games here. —*Richard Murphy, Painesville, OH* [5/1/77]

A: The Pan-American Games never were held at the Stadium, although there was an attempt to bring the games here. The other gent must be thinking of the special track meet held at the Stadium, August 21, 1931. The Stadium had just been opened and civic leaders invited the stars who had just finished competing in the Olympics at Los Angeles to stop in at the Stadium—all expenses paid, of course. It was part of a gala celebration with bands, dancers, etc.

Admission was free, therefore no actual turnstile count was available but the crowd estimate generally agreed on was 60,000 at the most. They saw a fine track show including a 100-yard dash around a curve between Jesse Owens and Eric

Brockmeyer of Germany, which Jesse won by two strides. He was timed at 9.6 seconds.

The biggest crowd ever for the Stadium sports event was 86,288 for the October 10, 1948 World Series game between the Indians and the Boston Braves. And nobody got in free.

GOOD HOUSEKEEPING

Q: When did fielders start bringing in their gloves after the third out? —*Scott's Barber Shop, Elyria, OH* [7/18/76]

A: This will come as a complete surprise to most present ball players, but until 1953 the players left their gloves on the field at the end of each inning. Infielders and outfielders would toss them on the outfield grass and if a ball hit the glove or a fielder tripped over one, the game went on as though the gloves weren't there.

As a player, Hank Greenberg rightfully thought it was ridiculous to leave the gloves on the field and turn it into an obstacle course. As general manager of the Indians, he was appointed to the rules committee in 1953 and finally convinced the other members that it would prove no great inconvenience to order the players to carry their gloves on and off the field.

Turned out he was right. Players have been good housekeepers ever since.

NOTABLE FIRST FOR MUDCAT

Q: When was the first time two black starting pitchers faced each other in the American League? Was it Mudcat Grant and Earl Wilson? —*Name Withheld* [4/18/76]

A: The first time it happened was April 15, 1961, when Mudcat *started* for the Indians against Bennie Daniels of the Washington Senators. The earliest two black pitchers *faced* each other in the American League was June 12, 1958. Again it was Grant going for the Indians against Connie Johnson of the Orioles. But this happened *during* the game, not at the start.

MORE NOTABLE FIRSTS

Q: Who were the first black coaches and pitchers in both the American League and National League? —*Name Withheld* [9/7/95]

A: The first pitchers were Dan Bankhead, Brooklyn Dodgers, 1947, and Satchel Paige, Cleveland Indians, 1948.

The first coaches were Jim Gilliam, Los Angeles Dodgers, 1965, and Elston Howard, New York Yankees, 1969.

I'm glad you didn't ask me a toughie, like who was the first black manager in the majors.

NO JOY IN MUDVILLE

Q: When does "Casey at the Bat" take place? Is it true? Was there such a player as Casey? —*Hall Perry, Lyndhurst, OH* [3/9/75]

A: It was written by Ernest L. Thayer as one of the series of ballads he was doing for the *San Francisco Examiner* under the by-line of "Phin." The Casey poem appeared Sunday, June 3, 1888. It was made famous by De Wolfe Hopper, an actor who recited it, with gestures, on the vaudeville stage. Thayer, a Harvard grad, grew up in Lawrence, Mass., which may have or may not have been Mudville. Indications are that it all came out of Thayer's vivid imagination and not from any particular incident, although it undoubtedly was triggered by several.

BABE, ON THE FLY

Q: Can you please inform me when the ground rule double came into effect? —*C.S. Stark, Cleveland, OH* [7/25/72]

A: In 1931. Prior to that, balls that bounced into the stands were home runs. But before I'm bombarded with letters about Babe Ruth's homers, all 60 he hit in 1927 made the seats *on the fly*.

PHUTILE PHILLIES

Q: Please verify for a friend of mine that a major league club with a .320 batting average for the season, including the batting average of the pitchers, wound up in the cellar. I think it was the Philadelphia Phillies of 1930, if I recall correctly. —*Bill Taylor, Parma Heights, OH* [5/11/75]

A: You were close. The 1930 Phillies had a team batting average of .315, which is much higher than most teams have today, even with designated hitters. Yet the Phillies finished dead last. Which shows how important pitching is.

·················· **"K" CLARIFICATION** ··················

Q: Recently I saw an article in another paper. A sentence read: "Joe DiMaggio struck out less than any slugger who ever lived—only 13 times in one season." I was surprised to read that, as I thought our friend Joey Sewell had a season record of only four. I called George Uhle, Joey's old teammate, and asked him. George also disagreed and mentioned a figure of seven maximum strikeouts for Sewell. I would appreciate having you set us straight on this record. —*Joseph A. Bender, Lakewood, OH* [6/9/75]

A: Sewell holds the record for fewest strikeouts. In 1925 he fanned only four times and he tied his own record in 1929 with another four-strikeout season. There are many others who fanned fewer than 13 times. Indians' manager Lou Boudreau, in leading the team to the pennant in 1948, struck out only nine times.

But the sentence you read was *not* wrong. The key word is "slugger". Sewell was *not* a slugger. Neither was Boudreau nor any of the others who struck out so seldom. DiMaggio hit plenty of home runs during this career. And for a slugger 13 strikeouts is indeed a feat.

ASIDE TO READERS: In this column Sunday, someone named "John Findley," an ex-Indian, was listed as having had six hits in six at-bats. April 29, 1952. I typed "Jim Fridley," the correct name. Somehow the electronic optical scanner that reads this copy and feeds it to a computer refused to believe Fridley did it. Either that or the machine has a friend named Findley.

·················· **MANY MOONS AGO** ··················

Q: I believe a few months ago I read in your column that among those who had made triple plays were a couple of first basemen. How is it possible to make an unassisted triple play from first base, or did I read you wrong? —*Rev. L. Perry* [10/29/63]

A: You read me right. Johnny Neun, Tigers first baseman, completed one against the Indians, May 31, 1927. That was many, many moons ago. He caught Homer Summa's liner, ran over and tagged Charley Jamieson between first and second and then tagged second base before Glenn Myatt could get back. Some moons earlier, in 1923, George Burns, playing first base for the Red Sox, completed an unassisted triple play in almost identical manner against—whom else?—the Indians.

When the moon is right the Indians become moonstruck.

················· **HOW JOE'S STREAK ENDED** ·················

Q: I know Joe DiMaggio's 56-game hitting streak was stopped by the Cleveland Indians. I know Ken Keltner made two great plays. Please tell me who was the starting pitcher and who was the relief pitcher and how many innings did they pitch. I say the stoppers were Al Smith and Kenny Keltner. —*Robert Owens, Marion, OH* [2/24/76]

A: Joe's streak was stopped at the Stadium, July 17, 1941. Al Smith started for the Indians and went 7⅓ innings. During that period Keltner made two fine plays on DiMaggio. Smith also walked him once. In the eighth the Yanks loaded the bases and Jim Bagby came in to replace Smith. There was one out. DiMaggio hit one in the hole between second and third. Lou Boudreau, positioned perfectly, slid to his right and turned the grounder into an inning-ending double play.

The next day Joe began a new streak that lasted 16 games. Now he's making a hit with Mr. Coffee.

················· **NO SUNDAY BASEBALL?** ·················

Q: Years ago, when Philadelphia outlawed Sunday baseball, Connie Mack used to bring 12 or 13 players to play Cleveland on Sunday. The Wheeling and Lake Erie Railroad used to run excursions and we enjoyed quite a few Sundays at League Park. But wasn't professional baseball outlawed on Sundays in Cleveland, too, at one time? I seem to remember a cartoon carried either in *The Plain Dealer* or the *Cleveland Leader* showing a ball marked "Sunday baseball" sailing over the fence and the cartoon was captioned, "Over the fence and out." —*Armin A. Ruof, Brewster, OH* [6/16/76]

A: Sunday baseball was banned here until 1911. The first Sunday game was played on May 14th of that year at League Park.

Connie Mack occasionally brought small squads here long after the ban was lifted on Sunday ball. On quick trips Connie sought to save railroad fare and meal money. Can you imagine what the players' union would do if a club tried to do that now?

·················· **BOTTOM OF THE TOP** ··················

Q: What was the lowest average to win the batting crown in the American or National League? —*Barney McCoy, Warren, OH* [2/9/89]

A: In 1968, Carl Yastrzemski won the American League crown with a .301 mark. Even so, he beat out his nearest rival, Danny Cater, by 11 points. The National League low came this past season when Tony Gwynn won with a .313 mark. Here's an oddity: Elmer Flick, the Hall of Fame great who was born in Bedford and played for the Indians, won the title in 1905 at .306 and, in doing so, lowered his lifetime average, which had been .315.

·················· **LEAGUE PARK PRICES** ··················

Q: I would like to know the price paid for general admission or grandstand seats at old League Park during the 1920 season. —*Frank Cox, Lorain, OH* [9/9/89]

A: A newspaper ad appearing April 11, 1920, gave these prices: Grandstand $1, Pavilion 75 cents, Bleachers 50 cents. And for those prices fans got to see the Indians win the pennant that year.

·················· **LEFT IS RIGHT** ··················

Q: The other evening I was viewing the movie, *Field of Dreams*. It depicted Shoeless Joe Jackson. In one scene it had him catching fly balls. He was left-handed. When he came to the plate for batting practice he batted right-handed. This baffled me because I've always stated that left-handed throwers who bat right-handed don't usually make good hitters. And Jackson was an outstanding hitter. Did they make a boo-boo in the film? —*Jim Everhart, New Philadelphia, OH* [9/29/90]

A: The real Shoeless Joe batted left-handed and threw right-handed, so he didn't shoot down your theory. Since the "Field of Dreams" was a fantasy perhaps this "mistake" was part of the fantasy. In any event, it was incorrect.

·················· **LOU BOUDREAU TRICKED** ··················

Q: Regarding the Indians' opening game, April 1945, against the Chicago White Sox. Please may I have the answer to three questions on the hidden ball trick played on Lou Boudreau: What base was he picked off? Who was the Indians' coach at that base? What Chicago player was involved? What inning? —*George F. Kimbel, Elyria, OH* [5/4/75]

A: In the sixth inning Boudreau, the Indians' player-manager, doubled and took third on an outfield fly. After the throw to third, Chisox third baseman Tony Cuccinello hid the ball in his glove. After Lou stepped off the base, Cuccinello tagged him, looked up at umpire Cal Hubbard and said, "How about it?" Neither Hubbard nor third base coach Burt Shotton had seen Cuccinello hide the ball.

"He's out if you've got the ball," said Hubbard.

Cuccinello showed it to him and a sheepish Boudreau walked off the field.

·················· **HISTORY OF THE SAC FLY** ··················

Q: A few questions about the sacrifice fly: 1. Was there a time when there was no such thing as a sacrifice fly? 2. Was there a time when a sacrifice fly was only credited when a run scored as a direct result? 3. What is the rule today on the sacrifice fly? —*Johny Pokky, Cleveland, OH* [3/13/83]

A: Here is its history: There was no such rule until 1908. Beginning then a batter received credit for a sacrifice fly when his caught fly to the outfield scored a runner from third. On a sacrifice fly the batter was credited with a run batted in but not charged with a time at bat. In 1926 the rule was expanded to include flies that advanced *any* runner.

In 1931 the entire sacrifice fly rule was dropped. It was restored in 1939, but only for run-scoring flies. In 1940 the rulemakers threw it out again.

In 1954 they made up their minds, apparently permanently, and restored the rule as it is written today. Here it is: "Score a sacrifice fly when, before two are out, the batter hits a fly ball or a line drive handled by an outfielder running to the outfield which (1) is caught and the runner scores after the catch or (2) is dropped and the runner scores, if in the scorer's judgment the runner could have scored after the catch had the fly ball been caught."

PHONY TALE

Q: We were having a discussion at work concerning the origin of the seventh-inning stretch. One of my co-workers tells me that it started in 1920 when Ray Chapman, Cleveland shortstop, was killed by a pitched ball. He says that Chapman was killed during the seventh inning and all the fans would stand up every game at that inning to pay honor to the fallen shortstop. I have never heard the story before. Could you shed any light on this matter? —*Dick Ovacek* [4/17/71]

A: The light exposes this story as a complete phony. The pitch that killed Chapman came in the *fifth* inning, not the seventh.

THE MOST-ASKED QUESTION

Q: Principal Paul says Mickey Mantle once hit a baseball over the roof and out of the park at Cleveland Stadium. I say he did not, nor has any other human being. Can you please settle this? Also, has anyone ever hit a home run out of Cleveland Stadium between left and right center field? —*Mike Popelas, Mentor* [7/22/89]

A: We haven't had this question in a while, so I thought we finally had convinced everybody that nobody, but nobody, ever hit a fair fly ball into the center-field bleachers, let alone out of the Stadium. Let's go over this once more: No batter ever has hit a home run on the fly into the permanent bleachers. And, of course, nobody ever has hit one out of the Stadium. There have been foul balls that have gone over the roof and landed outside the park. But a fair ball? Never. And it never will. This is the Stadium's 57th birthday for baseball and no ball has yet to reach the bleachers on the fly. Unless there's a hurricane, one never will. That goes for non-human beings too. Got it, Principal Paul?

8

Trumped Umps

Questions about Umpires and their Calls

Q: Batter hits a bouncing ball down the third base line. The ball goes over the bag about three feet high and continues into foul territory all the way to the left field fence. The home plate umpire called it a fair ball after the third base ump called it foul. Whose call is it? I maintain that the plate umpire's jurisdiction on this play goes up to third base and the third base ump's call includes third base and beyond. I lost the argument and the game by a home plate umpire who said, "I can change any call because I am the home plate umpire." I told him, "No way." Did I tell him right? —*Gene Kulik, Maple Heights* [7/13/75]

A: In the majors the plate umpire has jurisdiction *up to the base.* From the base and beyond the call belongs to the base umpire. If there is conflict on a play such as you describe the base ump's call becomes the official one. If there is a protest because of the difference in judgment the league president will rule in favor of the base ump if the ball has reached the bag and or gone beyond it.

  On your play it would be ruled a foul ball and all the screaming by the plate umpire can't change it, even though, as you describe it, the ball should have been called fair by the base ump.

  Finally, the plate ump has no right or authority to overrule a base empire's call when the plate umpire doesn't have jurisdiction over the play unless the base ump asks him to make a decision.

Tell that plate ump Hitler is dead.

NO NO CALL

Q: In a recent softball game a "no call" by the umpire cost my team a possible victory. The score was tied in the bottom of the last inning, the team at bat had a runner on second, one out. The batter swung and chopped the ball in front of the plate and unintentionally hit the ball a second time with his bat which was still in his grasp. As a result the ball was deflected away from the charging pitcher. The umpire made no call, leaving runners on first and third. A sacrifice fly followed and the result was a one-run loss. What's the call? What if the bat had split and the flying portion hit the ball? —*Jim Holmes, Fairfield, OH* [8/29/85]

A: The ump blew it. What you describe is an obvious "second hit," clearly covered by the rules. The batter is out, the ball is dead. There should have been two outs, with the runner remaining on second. If you didn't protest, you made a mistake. If the bat had split and the flying portion hit the ball, the ump would have been right in making "no call," for in that case the ball would have remained in play. But this was a "whole" bat and he had to call it.

JUDGMENT CALL

Q: We have a small wager bet on this: A friend said that an error cannot be charged to a fielder unless he touches the ball, but I say that if a *routine* fly ball is hit to an outfielder and he misjudges it and it falls near him that should be an error. What do you say? —*Ed Baker, Bedford, OH* [6/17/70]

A: I say I'd have to see the play in order to call it. An error can be charged to a fielder whether or not he touches the ball if, in the scorer's judgment, he should have caught it.

Here's the rule: It is not necessary that the fielder touch the ball to be charged with an error. "If . . . a pop fly falls untouched and in the scorer's judgment the fielder could have handled the ball with ordinary effort, an error shall be charged."

But if a fielder misjudges the ball it's not necessarily an error. There's no column on the score sheet for mental mistakes, although perhaps there should be.

That's why I'd have to see the play to call it.

SAFE, THEN OUT

Q: In a hotly contested baseball game, there was a close play at the plate. The runner was called safe. This infuriated the catcher, so he vehemently protested. The umpire immediately threw him out of the game. The catcher threw the ball down and argued a little more. During the argument, the batter-runner ran to second and then third, not knowing if time was out. The manager of the team in the field argued that the runner had to go back to first since time was automatically out at the ejection of the catcher. The umpire disagreed and said nobody called time, so the runner could advance at his own risk. Was he right? —*Michael Vogt, Dover* [8/19/89]

A: When a player is thrown out while a play is in progress, he is not officially ejected until the play is completely over. The ball remains in play until time is called. The ump was right. The batter-runner stays at the third and now the catcher can pack up his gear and his temper and leave quietly.

DOUBLE DIP

Q: Recently in a game which I was umpiring, one of the strangest plays happened. Not once, but twice. The batter hit a fly ball to short left center. The center fielder ran in to catch the ball. The ball bounced out of her glove and the shortstop caught the ball before it hit the ground. I ruled the batter safe in both cases. Was I correct? —*Randy Henzes, Peckville, PA* [7/8/79]

A: No. If the ball is held securely before reaching the ground, it's a legal catch and the batter is out. Thus you were wrong twice.

·························· **TIME . . . OUT** ··························

Q: When leading off an inning in men's softball I hit a grounder to deep shortstop. The throw got past the first baseman and bounced off the fence parallel with the base line. The ground rules are that the ball hitting on the bench side of a painted post was out of play. After reaching first base, I looked to the umpire to see if I was awarded second. He then called, "Time out." I assumed I was awarded second base and proceeded to walk to it. The ball was thrown to the second baseman who tagged me. The same umpire who had just called "time" called me out. Was his call correct? —*Roger Carey, Cleveland, OH* [7/21/81]

A: Absolutely not. When time is out it is impossible to record an out. This guy probably is still calling plays while he's driving home after the game is over.

······················· Out of Left Field ·······················

Q: When Bill Belter of the San Diego Wharf Rats slides just under the tag of Wilmington Deckhands' third baseman, Grant Glover, the play is so close the umpire's call of safe evokes a brief but tumultuous rhubarb. With so many players milling about and discussing it nose-to-nose with the umpire, he doesn't notice that Glover didn't immediately return the ball to the pitcher, but hid it somewhere under his arm—the old hidden ball trick. By the time the uproar subsides, the pitcher has resumed his position on the rubber and stands glaring at the next batter as if to deliver the next pitch, inspiring Belter to get up, brush himself off and take a lead-off down the third base line. At this moment, Glover whips out the ball and makes a lunging tag on Belter while the surprised umpire signals "out." Now we instantly have another magilla raging as Gus Gruesome, the Wharf Rats' manager, and Ivan (The Terrible) Zarr, the Wharf Rats' third base coach, perform an elaborate rock and roll dance in front of the umpire while explaining that Belter should be entitled to score because the pitcher balked by taking the mound as if to pitch while not actually in possession of the ball. Considering that you, the umpire, already have ruled Belter out, what now is your position? —*Robert Dell, Cleveland Heights, OH* [8/13/78]

A: One of embarrassment because the Rats are right. It is a balk. The pitcher can't step on the rubber without the ball when runners are on base. But the plate umpire quickly would call balk on this play, getting the third base ump out of the dance.

Incidentally, a good ump would have called time during the initial rhubarb. And once time is called, it's impossible to employ the hidden ball trick, for play does not resume until the pitcher assumes pitching position *with* the ball.

The manager and the coach appear to be a gruesome twosome.

HOMER CALL

Q: Runners on first and second, two outs. The batter hits a long fly to the outfield. On the ball's downward flight it hits the top of the plywood fence and bounces over for what everyone thought was a home run. I called it a double because the rule says for it to be a home run the ball must clear the barrier on the fly. I have been umpiring for 15 years and this is the first time I have seen this. Was I correct? —*Mike Shannon, Lyndhurst, OH* [11/28/98]

A: I can understand your confusion because the rule is somewhat unclear. But every umpire in the majors would call this a home run. In fact, they are told to do so. When the ball hits the top of the fence and bounces over it, it is considered to have cleared the barrier. So if in the next 15 years you see a ball hit the very top of the fence and bounce over, call it a homer.

QUICK HOOK

Q: Can an umpire forfeit a game simply because he is assaulted? Unfortunately, this happened in our Senior Little League to one of our umpires after he called a balk and the pitcher threw a tantrum and was ejected. The manager came out of the dugout and blindsided the umpire, who then forfeited the game. —*B. R., New Haven, CT* [3/6/99]

A: Officials at Little League headquarters in Williamsport, Pa., say the umpire should have ejected the manager from the game and the grounds, but not called an immediate forfeit. If the manager refused after a given length of time, then a forfeit should have been declared. After the game the ump should make out a written report to the league president who, with the approval of his board of directors, no doubt would dismiss the manager permanently. Then the ump could prefer charges against the manager in court. I hope he did. But immediate forfeiture was not the correct way to go, because it isn't fair to the players who were behaving properly.

·························· **FORCE IS OFF** ··························

Q: This happened during our Colt game. Men on first and third, one out. A fly ball was hit to our right fielder. The man on third tagged up, but the runner on first ran when the ball was hit, thinking there were two outs. The right fielder caught the ball, then threw home but the runner was safe at the plate. Finally, after realizing the runner on first was between second and third and didn't tag up, the catcher threw to first base for the double play. The umpire ruled that the run counted because the right fielder threw home first. Our coach and I thought the run shouldn't have scored just as long as we get the force out for the double play. Was the umpire correct in his decision?
—*Walter Wellstead, Jr., Perrysburg, OH* [8/8/78]

A: The ump was correct in allowing the run to count but not for the reason you say he gave. The run counts because it scored before the third out on a play in which the third out was *not* a force.

The runner on first didn't have to go anywhere. Therefore, he wasn't forced.

May the force be with you next time.

·························· **KILLING A BALL** ··························

Q: I'm an umpire and in a game I was watching, this happened. I would like to know what the ruling is: Runner on second. Passed ball. Runner goes to third. Runner is safe. Ball gets away from third baseman and goes behind umpire. No one knows where the ball is and no time is called. Umpire goes to his pocket and throws new ball to the pitcher and then picks up the live ball and puts it in his pocket. I say ball is still in play and everyone else seems to agree the ump was right. —*D. J. M., Sharon, PA* [10/30/75]

A: The ump was totally wrong, of course, in picking up the live ball and putting another in play. But since no bases were being run at the time and all play had ceased, his actions were tantamount to calling the ball dead.

But had he done it while the action had been continuing, he might have felt like killing himself because what he did was an absolute no-no.

·························· **NO APPEAL** ····························

Q: On a "checked swing," must the home plate umpire check with the first or third base umpire if the manager insists? In other words, can the plate umpire call "ball" or "strike" and ignore the request for an appeal? —*Bruce Wachsman, Mansfield, OH* [5/6/89]

A: If the plate umpire calls "strike," there can be no appeal. It's a strike. But the ump calls "ball" on a checked swing and the catcher requests the base umpire for his view, that request must be granted. And if the base ump says the bat crossed the plate, the plate ump must reverse himself and call it a strike. For right-handed batters the appeal is to the first base ump and for left-handers the third base ump makes the call.

··················· **Out of Left Field** ····················

Q: Is it possible for a base runner in the majors to change an umpire's call in this unusual way: Runner slides into a base and is called safe, but he knows he really was tagged out. Being honest, he tells the umpire. Can the ump change his call? —*Shawn Trueman, Sandusky, OH* [7/14/88]

A: Absolutely. The ump always can change his call if he is convinced he's wrong. If he does reverse himself in the case you present, I can hear the teammates of the player saying, "Who do you think you are, George Washington?"

················· **UMPING IS FUN!** ·················

Q: In a recent CYO baseball game I was forced into being an umpire when the umpires for our game failed to show. Please settle this disputed call: Runners on first and second, one out. Batter hits to short, runner on second runs into shortstop, allowing the ball to go through. I claim the runner was out for interference. He made no attempt to avoid the fielder. The opposing manager claimed the base paths belong to the runner and he's allowed to do it. Who is correct? —*Randy Russell, University Heights, OH* [5/11/75]

A: The runner *must* avoid the fielder who is attempting to field a batted ball. The base paths belong to the fielder *not* the runner, in this instance.

In fact, on your play, if you think the interference broke up a double play you could call both the runner *and* the batter out.

Umpiring is fun, huh?

················· **UMP BUMPED** ·················

Q: I was the catcher. There was a runner on first. After the pitch I tried to throw the ball back to the pitcher but the plate umpire accidentally bumped me. My throw went wild and the runner advanced to second. The umpire allowed him to remain there. Was he right? —*Craig Evans, Madison, OH* [6/2/90]

A: No. The umpire should have declared the ball dead immediately and ordered the runner to return to first base. And it would have been nice if he had said, "So sorry," to you.

················· **MEETING ADJOURNED** ·················

Q: At a recent meeting several umpires in Little League programs were present. One umpire asked the following question: A runner was on third when the batter hit a fly ball to center. The runner came in and touched home plate, but somehow got the idea that the ball had been caught and he returned to third. The ball was dropped. The ball was thrown into the infield, but by then the runner had safely returned to third. Two of the umpires said the runner should have been sent to the dugout and allowed to score because he had touched home plate. Two

others said that because the player had voluntarily returned to third he had to remain there and no run would be scored. Who was correct? We can't start our next meeting until we find out.
—*John Looper, Westlake, OH* [8/18/88]

A: Once a runner legally tags home plate any further actions on his part can't nullify his run. There is a special rule on this. Remove the runner off third base. He already had scored. The run counts. Start your next meeting.

······························ **BOXED IN** ·····························

Q: Batter is hit by a batted ball while standing in the batter's box. The ball then bounced into fair territory and the batter runs to first, reaching it safely. The ump allows him to remain there. Right or wrong? —*W. R.* [7/4/72]

A: Wrong. It became a foul ball and was dead the instant it hit the batter while he was still in his box. The ump put himself in a box with this one.

··················· **TWO WRONGS, NO RIGHTS** ··················

Q: Manager sitting on the bench calls out to the pitcher, "Keep it low on this guy." Umpire points finger at manager and says, "That's one trip to the mound." Is he right? Another situation: Manager calls "time." Umpire grants it and manager goes out to mound to consult with his pitcher. The manager heads back to the bench. Before reaching the foul line he turns a couple of steps toward the pitcher and shouts something else to him. The umpire says, "That's your second trip. Your pitcher comes out." Will you comment, please, for the benefit of both managers and umpires in our league. Use major league rules as the basis. —*Paul E. Lucas, Akron, OH* [7/2/78]

A: Yelling is *not* a trip. The ump was wrong in both instances. The purpose of the rule is to prevent the delays caused by trips to the mound. When a manager lets his lips do his walking, the pitcher's status is not in jeopardy.

.... **THE UMP KILLED IT** ....

Q: Our batter tried to get out of the way of a pitch, but it hit the knob of his bat and rolled into fair territory. The umpire yelled "Foul ball," then realized he was wrong and yelled, "Fair ball. Play it." Our batter stopped the instant he heard "Foul ball," but when the catcher heard the call reversed he threw it to first base for the out. This doesn't seem fair. Was it? —*Alex Mack, Mansfield, OH* [8/14/98]

A: Interpreters on all levels—high school, college and the majors —say in this case the umpire killed the play, actually ruling it a dead ball when he initially yelled, "Foul ball." The batter should return to the plate and continue his at-bat.

.... **STILL WONDERING** ....

Q: This play occurred in a baseball game in Fremont about 12 years ago and I've never had it clarified: Men on first and second. A screamer is hit toward third. The third baseman moves to his right and behind the bag. The ball, however, hit the third base bag and came to rest on the second-base side of it. The runner on second, anticipating a close play, had begun his slide. He slid into the ball which was sitting between him and the bag.

　　The defense claimed the man was out because this was a batted ball that had been neither previously touched nor had gone past an infielder. As an umpire I called the man safe. I'm still wondering. —*Duke Ziebold, Genoa, OH* [4/25/67]

A: You should have called the runner out for being hit by a batted ball before it passed a fielder. But don't eat your heart over it. I put this play to a couple of major league umpires and they kicked it around plenty before making the right call.

.... **NO, NO, AND NO** ....

Q: This is in regards to a televised game I saw recently between the Kansas City Royals and the Oakland A's. The A's were winning 2-0 in the seventh. The Royals were at bat and had a runner on first. The batter grounded to the first baseman who threw to second to start what he hoped would be a double play.

The second baseman ran to the bag, touched it with his foot, then *took his foot off the bag and caught the ball.* The umpire called the runner out and the throw back to first was too late to complete the double play. The next man tripled, scoring the runner from first. The Royals finally lost the game, 2-1.

At first I thought I was seeing things, but a replay was shown. I had a chance to look closely and I was correct, although the announcers didn't catch it. Had the umpire called the runner safe at second the score would have been tied by the triple.

Two questions: One—if the Royals had known of the umpire's error could they have protested? Two—is there some sort of mutual agreement among umpires and players allowing this leeway on-base tagging at second?

I think the Royals were cheated. Would writing a letter to them help in any way? —*Bill Mallardi, Akron, OH* [5/11/69]

A: The answer to all your questions is *no.* There can be no protest on an umpire's judgment call. There is no "leeway" or understanding on phantom tags. Fielders are supposed to tag the bases while the ball is in their possession. I have seen many runners called "safe" when the second baseman or shortstop tries to gain a step by cheating on this play. And forget about the letter. You would be wasting a stamp.

The umpire called the play as he saw it—without benefit of instant replay. And who's to say whether the camera had a better angle than he did? You?

························ **STRUCK UMP** ························

Q: A base runner was between second and third base when the second baseman threw the ball over the third baseman's head striking the umpire. The third baseman recovered the ball in time to tag the runner. As umpire, I called him out. Right? —*John A. Fitzgerald, Cleveland Heights, OH* [3/15/65]

A: Right. The ball remains in play. An umpire is just like a stone on the field, but no one had better call him a rockhead.

································ **FORCE OFF, UMP RIGHT** ····················

Q: One out, runners on first and second. Ball grounded sharply to second. Runner on first, seeing he would be tagged out by second baseman, returns to first base. Second baseman throws to first baseman and first baseman has his foot on the base when he catches the ball. He tags out runner, who is still standing on first. Umpire rules batter out and runner standing on first safe because the batter, by being out, removed the force play. The other team protested the call, saying both are out. How do you see it? —*Jerry Beale, Toledo, OH* [8/2/80]

A: Exactly as the umpire did, because he was right.

····················· **CORRECTIBLE ERROR** ····················

Q: Man on third base, score tied, last half of the last inning. Batter hits ground ball to second baseman. Throw to first baseman is high. First baseman jumps, catches ball and comes down on the bag before the runner. Umpire calls runner safe and the runner from third scores. Argument ensues. Within seconds umpire says he blew the call but he would not change it. Question: can a protest be made on a judgment call since umpire, within seconds, admitted blowing it? —*Kenneth Callahan, Euclid, OH* [6/23/75]

A: Unfortunately no. A protest can be registered on a mistake in the rules, but *not* on a judgment call. You can notify the head of the league that the ump admitted his mistake but wouldn't change his decision. If the ump admits this to his superiors he should be reprimanded or fired.

The umpire's job is to make the *correct* decision even if he has to reverse himself to do so. It takes guts to be an ump. A good one has the courage to admit he was wrong, correct himself, and take the heat. But he'll have a clear conscience.

····················· **WHEN YA GOTTA GO . . .** ····················

Q: Would you please give me the information on the number of times a player or manager can be thrown out of a baseball game per team in the American League? —*Ken Gerlock, Maple Heights, OH* [5/5/63]

A: Here's a case where one out per game is all you get. When the umpire says you gotta go, you gotta go.

JUST DO IT

Q: This play was thrown around at our recent umpire's meeting. What is your call? Batter bunts ball. Ball rolls back and hits bat in fair territory. In the umpire's judgment it was definitely unintentional that the ball hit the bat a second time. After ball hits bat the second time, it then rolls foul. The question: is it a fair or foul ball. We had about 50-50 answers. —*Don Miklich, Cleveland, OH* [4/24/67]

A: There can be only one answer. It's a fair ball. Moreover, any major league umpire would call the batter out even though you say the ball hit the bat a second time *unintentionally*. Here's a tip: Don't try to be a mind reader. The batter shouldn't drop his bat in the field of play. If he does and the ball hits it a second time causing it to be deflected from its normal path the burden is on the batter. Call him out for interference.
  And don't take a vote. Just do it.

ONE-MAN JOB

Q: Please give me the ruling on this particular play in slow-pitch. A man on second and third and one out. Batter hits a fly to left. The ball is caught. Both runners tag up and leave simultaneously. The runner from second is thrown out at third for the third out. Does the run count? —*Ben J. Maulorico,* [6/9/67]

A: This is strictly a judgment call. If the umpire thinks a runner from third tagged home plate before the third out was made the run counts. Thus there is only one man who has the answer to your question—the umpire.

JUST RIDICULOUS

Q: A runner on third left too soon, in our opinion, after a catch. The pitcher got the ball, said this to the umpire, "We're appealing the runner who was on third. He left too soon." Our pitcher stepped off the rubber and threw to the third baseman who tagged the bag. The ump refused to recognize the appeal, saying it has to be made by a fielder, not the pitcher. We protested. Should we have won the protest? —*Name Withheld* [6/11/74]

A: If you didn't, the arbitration board pulled a rock. Your team made a perfectly proper appeal. I suppose the umpire read the definition of an appeal. ("An appeal is the act of a fielder in claiming violation of the rules by the offensive team.") and he decided the pitcher isn't a fielder. If he reads further in Rule 2.00 he'll note, "A *fielder* is any defensive player."

Of all the ridiculous calls I've heard in the past few weeks this one is tops and if the arbitration board didn't overrule the ump they topped him.

·············· BAGS REMAIN JUICED ··············

Q: At the meeting of the Amherst Umpires Association this question came up. It took place in a high school game last year.

Bases are loaded with one out. The ball is hit to the second baseman. The runner interferes with the second baseman by running into him. Interference is called. The second baseman recovers in time to throw the runner out at first base resulting in a double play. Is this correct or is the ball dead? Do the runners advance if the ball is dead, resulting in one run and men left on first and third and two outs? —*M. D. Paton, Amherst, OH* [4/24/63]

A: In this multiple choice of answers you left out the only correct one. The ball is dead the instant the interference took place. The runner who interfered is out, making it two outs. *And the bases remain loaded.* You see, the runner who was on third stays there. The batter gets first base, forcing the runner who was there to move to second. Of course you see. You're the umpire.

·············· UMP PUNCH ··············

Q: Can an umpire ever get kicked out a game for punching a player? —*Bill Arthur, Rocky River, OH* [4/28/63]

A: No, but after the game he can be suspended or fired by the league president. Though he can't be kicked out during the game, he's in danger of being knocked out.

······················· **THAT'S A BALL** ·······················

Q: Here is a situation that happens quite frequently in our slow-pitch league. The pitch is lobbed toward the plate and very obviously is going to drop on home plate at the back point. If it drops down on the plate it is a ball. But the catcher sticks his glove over the plate and catches the ball before it hits the plate and the ump calls it a strike. I disagree with this call. Who's right? —*Bill Wiencek, N. Royalton, OH* [5/4/75]

A: If a pitch hits home plate, it's a ball. Therefore, if I'm umpiring the game I'm not going to let the catcher call the pitches for me. If, in my judgment, the ball would have landed on the plate, I would call it a ball. And if I were the hitter, I'd reach down and touch the catcher's glove each time he sticks it over the plate. That would be catcher's interference and I'd trot to first base. Maybe I'd even run.

······················· **FARAWAY EYES** ·······················

Q: Slow-pitch softball, but I also would like a ruling if it had been baseball. Man on first, no outs. The batter hits the ball in the hole at short. The shortstop makes the play at second base, committing no fielding or throwing error. The runner from first base beats the throw to second. The argument is the scoring. Some would have the batter hitting into a fielder's choice, regardless if he is safe or out. Others say the fielder's choice is scored only if the force is made, or on an error. —*Barry Johnson, Dallas, TX* [7/20/75]

A: This is strictly a scorer's judgment call. If he thinks the shortstop could have thrown out the batter, it becomes a fielder's choice. If he believes the shortstop had no chance to get the batter, it's a hit. In this case, judging by your description, I'm calling it a base hit from almost 2,000 miles away.

······················· **ALL SET!** ·······················

Q: I am an umpire in Sharon, Pa. I had a fellow umpire explain a decision on a play he had last season with which we cannot agree. A batter is up; he gets a single. The next man is up. The ball is pitched. The batter does not swing. The runner on first begins to steal second on the pitch. For some reason he stops between first and second. The catcher throws to second and the runner is caught in a rundown situation. As the runner is on his way back to first, the second baseman throws the ball over the first baseman's head and it goes out of bounds.

The umpire awarded the runner second and third base. I disagree. I say he should get only second. What is the correct ruling on the play? —*Charles Perell, Farrell, PA* [5/31/75]

A: He is awarded two bases beyond the last one he touched at the time of the overthrow. The other umpire was correct on his call. The runner gets third base.

Now you're all set for the summer. Happy umpiring.

.... **BATTLE OF THE UMPS** ....

Q: I was recently umpiring a ball game. The batter hit a single to right field and overran first base. He then turned into the playing field and walked back toward first. The right fielder ran in and tagged him before he reached the base. I called him out, but the home plate umpire disagreed. He said the runner had not made a break toward second and he overruled me. Was I right or wrong? —*George Wildeman, Mentor, OH* [7/18/76]

A: If you called the runner out because, in your opinion, he *did* make a break for second. You were right. But if you called him out just because he turned left instead of right, you were wrong.

A runner must make a break for second in order to become vulnerable to a tag. A deep turn into the playing field would constitute a break in my book. But the mere turn to the left and the immediate return to the bag is no break.

You had jurisdiction over the call and the plate ump should not have entered into it unless you asked his opinion.

Still, I can't fault him if it was obvious to him you misunderstood the rule. I hope he talked with you privately and that you agreed to the reversal of your decision.

Umps never should fight each other. They have enough trouble with the players.

········· **NICE AND RIGHT, TOO** ··········

Q: This play came up in our Little League game the other night.
Runners on first and third, one out. Batter hits ball between
first and second, striking runner. Umpire calls him out but
allows the runner from third to score. He said that the runner
was three-fourths of the way home so he is allowed to score. I
say it's a dead ball and the run can't score. Who is right? Please
print without my name and the city because this umpire is
probably our most knowledgeable one and I would not want to
embarrass him. —E. G. [8/8/76]

A: You're a nice man. You also are correct. The ball is dead, no
runners can advance. The batter gets first base and is credited
with a single.
    Perhaps now the umpire is more knowledgeable.

·········· **WAVERING UMP** ···········

Q: I am manager of the Massillon entry in the Canton Class A
League. In the sixth inning the batter, with a two-and-two
count, made a swing and the home plate umpire called, "Strike
three—out." To my surprise the batter told the umpire that he
had a half-swing and the umpire, after conferring with the
base umpire, put the count at three and two. I immediately
protested the game. I have seen repeatedly, in the majors,
catchers ask the home plate umpire to appeal to other umpires
on the half-swing but I have never seen a batter or the offensive team ask for an appeal. In 32 years as a player, a manager,
and coach, I never have protested an umpire's judgment call,
but I believe in this case I have a valid reason and would like
your opinion. —*Augustin Mayor, Massillon, OH* [7/17/77]

A: This is a dandy, Mr. Mayor, and I don't blame you for protesting mightily. The rule specifically says a strike call can't be
appealed by anybody. It's the plate ump's call exclusively. Only
when a half-swing is called a *ball* can the defensive team ask
for a second opinion.
    The plate umpire was guilty of horrible mechanics. He didn't
know the rule and he didn't have the courage of his convic-
tions. He should *not* have asked anybody. If he called "strike"
that's what it should have been.

But since he did ask the base ump for help and since he did change his call after getting it, I'm afraid his final decision would have to stand. An umpire is entitled to change his decision, even on a judgment call, when he thinks he is wrong.

If this man doesn't believe in himself when the rules make it clear it must be his call, he should let the air out of his protector and get a non-decision making job.

······················· **FIRE THE UMP** ·······················

Q: Last season the following occurred. We were leading by a couple of runs late in a city softball league game. The other team was at bat. A ball was hit to our center fielder. He attempted to knock down the ball with his body and injured his hand in the process. After the play was completed we requested time to be granted so we could see if he could continue to play. If he wasn't then we would have made a substitution. The infield umpire was willing to grant time and tried to. The home plate umpire denied the request and said, "Play ball." Our pitcher was not willing to pitch until our injured player was tended to one way or another. Before we knew what was happening the umpire was saying, "Ball one, ball two, ball three, ball four, batter take your base." Throughout the incident the umpire was extremely belligerent. Players from both sides claimed the umpire used profane language when yelling at our pitcher, which only made matters worse. During the entire game the home plate umpire mentioned many times, "I've got somewhere else to be." Eventually, our pitcher was ejected. As he was leaving the field he threw a bag of softballs on the field. Because of this the umpire forfeited the game. Some governing body in the league decided that if we could prove the actions of one player (our pitcher) should not have resulted in a forfeit, then they would allow our protest. I don't understand this decision. We didn't protest the forfeit. We were protesting the actions of the home plate umpire. We felt the umpire instigated the whole situation by not allowing us time to tend to our injured player, by cussing our pitching and by his belligerent manner. Could this game have been rightfully protested? I know a judgment call is not grounds for protest. But does this come under the same category? And what action could we

have taken if we could not protest it? —*David Loeber, Lorain, OH*
[3/5/87]

A: The plate umpire was wrong in overruling the base umpire's
granting of time when your player was injured. All umpires
have equal authority in calling time and one *can't* overrule
another. Had you protested the plate umpire's actions on this
you would have had solid grounds for winning your case. The
umpire broke a *rule* when he vetoed the base umpire's call.

With respect to the plate umpire's ultimate decision, normally the ejection of one player isn't grounds for forfeit. But
your pitcher's subsequent actions, throwing the balls on the
field, could be construed as refusing to leave immediately when
ordered to do so. This *is* reason enough to call a forfeit. So this
becomes a judgment call. And judgments, unlike mistakes in
the rules, are not grounds for protest.

The umpire, based on your version, should be reprimanded
or fired by the league for his behavior. But your protest
wouldn't be upheld—unless you protested his dictatorial action
in illegally overruling the base umpire.

I surely would like to hear the plate umpire's side of the
story.

························ **HIGH FIVE** ························

Q: This happened in our slo-pitch softball game. Our runner had
an easy inside-the-park home run, but he was called out for
giving a "high five" to our third base coach. Doesn't the rule
require actual assistance of the runner and more than an inno-
cent handshake? —*Emmett McAuliffe, Niles, OH* [8/3/89]

A: The ump blew this one. The rulebook clearly says interference
by a coach requires aiding the runner. A "high five" more than
likely would slow down the runner, rather than help him. In
any case, a "high five" or a handshake shouldn't be penalized.

···················· **INFIELD FLY − IF FAIR** ····················

Q: The following baseball scenario has been under discussion for
a long time. Bases loaded. Pop-up in foul territory on a very
windy day. The umpire did not call "Infield fly." The ball came
down in fair territory and hit the runner standing on third

base in the head and the ball rolled to the shortstop. With no "infield fly" being called, all the runners started running. The shortstop threw home and forced out the runner from third. The catcher threw to third and forced the runner from second for a double play. What are the correct answers to the following questions: How do you correct an "infield fly" not called? What about the runner hit on the head? Were the runners required to run? —*Eugene W. Matty, Kirtland, OH* [1/11/03]

A: Of course, the umpire should have immediately called "infield fly"—if fair. But he didn't. And it's not an infield fly unless the umpire calls it one. The umpires have sole jurisdiction and judgment, by rule, on this play and if they blow it, it's *not* an infield fly. Therefore, the runner standing on third who was hit by the fair ball is out and the ball becomes dead immediately. In baseball, the base is not an island of safety, except on an infield fly. The batter is awarded first base, the other runners move up one base and the bases remain full. If the umpire had called "infield fly—if fair," as he should have, the batter would be out and the ball would be dead the instant it hit the runner on third. He is allowed to remain on third because on an infield fly the base does become a safe haven. The bases remain occupied by the same runners who were there originally.

·························· **IN THE DARK** ··························

Q: It's getting dark and the lights are just coming on and are still not bright. Pitcher throws curve which hits batter in the upper arm. He makes no move to get out of the way. Ump calls him out for not trying to get out of the way. Batter says he didn't see the ball. I say the ump was wrong. He should award the batter first base or at least it should be a strike or a ball. Who's right? —*Ralph Peachman, Avon Lake, OH* [4/30/88]

A: If, in the judgment of the umpire, the batter purposely allowed the ball to hit him the batter doesn't get first base. If the ball was in the strike zone he should call it a strike. If it was outside the strike zone it should be a ball. The ump was wrong in calling the batter out.

························ **WRONG, WRONG, WRONG** ····················

Q: In a recent Garfield Heights church league slow-pitch game this happened: Fast man on third, slow man on first, one out. Ground ball is hit to short. Out at second, Out at first. But speedy man on third crossed home plate before the runner is out at first. Ump says, "Double play. Run counts." We couldn't believe it. He says in baseball it wouldn't count, but in the Amateur Softball Association rules it does. I'm under the impression no runs can score when the third out of an inning is on the batter thrown out at first. Tell the ump he's wrong. We should have protested. As it was, we lost by one run. —*George Jana, Northfield Village, OH* [8/5/79]

A: Ump, you are *wrong*. The scoring rules are identified on all levels of baseball and softball. No run can score when the third out is made by the batter before he reaches first base.

Don't go into Mr. Jana's barber shop for a haircut, at least not for awhile. You might come out bald.

························ **THE RULE IS CLEAR** ····················

Q: The score is 4-3 in favor of the visiting team. Bottom half of the last inning, two outs with runner on second. Batter singles to center. Center fielder throws home. Runner from second is safe at the plate. The batter meanwhile had rounded second. The catcher throws to second and the batter breaks for third. The ball bounces away, but remains in play. The runner breaks for home. The third baseman throws home. There was no possible play at the plate because the home team was all around the plate. The ball landed somewhere in the crowd of players. The umpire called interference on the home team and sent the runner back to third. The next pitch was wild and the game ended with the winning run scoring from third. Wasn't the umpire wrong in sending the runner back to third? On an interference call isn't the runner out? The game took place in the Connie Mack tourney in Youngstown. —*Chris Maduri, Northfield, OH* [8/12/75]

A: Unless you didn't give me a full description of the play the umpire was totally wrong. If the ball was in play while the home team interfered with the play at the plate, the ump was obligated to call the runner out. He can't try to be a Solomon and send the runner back. The rule 7.09e, clearly states the runner is out.

Even Connie Mack, as gentle as he was, would have screamed about this call.

.... **MAKING NO CALL** ....

Q: This play occurred in a major league baseball game. Runner on third with no outs. Batter hits a grounder to short. The short-stop fires the ball to the catcher to try to nail the fleet-footed runner. The runner hook slides away from the tag but also misses the plate. The umpire stood motionless, not making a call. The catcher, seeing no call was made, scrambled after the runner whereupon the ump called the runner out after the tag was made. My friend says the ump did the proper thing by not making an initial call. I say he was wrong and must signal "safe" in order to prevent tipping off the defense that no tag was made. Who's correct? Two jellybeans are riding on this one. —*Steve Dockman, Parma, OH* [6/1/80]

A: For years umpiring organizations have been kicking this play around. About eight years ago the American and National Leagues and the minors finally got together and agreed to use identical mechanics on this play. They decided that since there was no tag of the player, and that the player did not tag the base, the umpire should make no call. I agree with you that this is tantamount to announcing to the world that the runner missed the base, and I would be in favor of having the umpire rule safe inasmuch as the runner is safe unless he is tagged out. But wiser heads have decided otherwise and now umpires are taught not to make any call at all. Then after the next pitch the umpire should designate to the official scorer that the run counts.

Sorry about the jellybeans.

.... **A MESS AT HOME** ....

Q: Runner on second, no outs. Batter singles to center. The throw comes home. Runner beats the throw home, but misses the plate. As he goes back he runs into the catcher. The umpire calls interference on the runner as the catcher was trying to make a play on the batter-runner who was now attempting to reach third. He ruled no run. Runner is out. Was this the correct call? —*Ken Gerber, Lorain, OH* [9/19/98]

A: He was incorrect when he nullified the run. When a runner passes a base, it is assumed he touched it unless there is an appeal. Since you now have a runner who scored inasmuch as no appeal was made on him, he is not out. But because the umpire ruled he interfered with the catcher's attempt to throw out the batter-runner, the batter-runner must be called out. So now you have one run and one out. But—and this is a big but —the defense hasn't lost its right to appeal the miss of home. If it does tag home, there would be two outs and the run would be erased.

················· **THE UMP WAS OUT OF ORDER** ················

Q: With two outs, a runner on second, and a 3-2 count on the batter, the runner attempts to steal third. The pitch is called ball four. The runner is thrown out attempting to steal, for the third out. The next inning the same batter who had walked to end the previous inning comes up. The pitcher throws one pitch, a called strike, and then appeals that the batter is out of order. The umpire rules that because the batter never reached first base before the runner was out stealing, he was batting properly. What is the ruling? —*David E. Kindle, Erie, PA* [5/25/91]

A: The ump was wrong. The batter completed his time at bat when ball four was called. The batter who follows him should have led off the next inning. When the appeal was made, the proper batter should have been ordered to bat with a count of one strike. If the appeal had come after the incorrect batter finished his turn, the proper batter would have been declared out and the batter who followed him now would be up. That is, if the umpire knew his rules.

···················· **PROTEST!** ····················

Q: A game is protested during the ninth inning and after the game the protest is filed improperly and the arbitration board upholds the protest. Now, am I correct in assuming the game should be continued from the point of the protest, with the incorrect call rectified and the game played to completion? Or is the whole game replayed? —*Brian V. Kochunas, Warren, OH* [6/20/76]

A: When a protest is upheld because an umpire made a mistake in the rules the game should be replayed from the point of the protest.

The official rules give no specifics for replaying protests, suggesting each league should establish its own code. But in the majors and all other leagues possessing some stature, the replay is always ordered from the point of protest. In your case it would be the ninth inning.

To wipe out what happened before would be unfair to the team that legally had taken the lead. And that's the purpose of league presidents, commissioners and arbitration boards—to be fair.

Fair enough?

9

The Errors of Their Ways

Fielding Follies

Q: While pitching in a softball game, the following play occurred: One out, runners on first and second. The ball was hit directly back to me. The force knocked my glove off and it landed upright with the ball still in it. I picked the ball out of the glove and threw it to first, doubling the runner, I thought. The umpire allowed only one out, that of the batter-runner, claiming the catch was illegal. I protested, stating that the glove was not detached, according to the rules, as it was forced off my hand not of my own volition. I have umpired for many years and can't find a rule covering this situation specifically. I say it was a legal catch and that the runner on first was doubled off because he had left his base. —*George R., Lorain, OH* [12/7/02]

A: It was not a legal catch. The definition of a catch covers it. You must hold the ball securely and have complete control of it long enough to establish full possession, in the judgment of the umpire. If the force of the hit knocks the glove and ball out of your hand you certainly don't have complete control of it. In your case, the glove maintained control, but you couldn't maintain control of your glove. Nice try. No catch.

························· **KNOWS HIS STUFF** ·······················

Q: Here's the situation: A long fly is hit and bounces once. The outfielder plays the bounce, but he bobbles the ball and it falls *over* the fence. When this occurred in a recent softball game the ump gave the batter a ground-rule double. He and his team contended that since the ball had been touched he should be allowed as many bases as he could get. Who's right? —*Keith McCown, Lakewood, OH* [7/1/70]

A: The umpire. He knows his rules. If the batter did, he wouldn't have argued.

·················· **Out of Left Field** ··················

Q: I have a videotape of baseball's unusual plays and one shows the third baseman on his hands and knees trying to blow a fair bunt into foul territory. Is it legal to blow on the ball to make it go foul? —*Mike Matoni, Warren, OH* [10/31/90]

A: No. The instant the player blows on a ball while it is in fair territory, it becomes a fair ball. It's the same as physically touching the ball. So save your breath.

·················· **TO HIS CHAGRIN** ··················

Q: In a recent Mets-Giants game, with one out, a Giants batter flied out to the left fielder, who thought his catch made it three outs. As he ran off the field he handed the ball to a small boy in the stands. When another fan held up two fingers the fielder suddenly realized there only were two outs, so he ran back to the boy, snatched the ball out of his hand, and threw it into the infield as the runners on base were advancing. If one of them had been tagged out, would the out have counted? —*Ray Nicholson, West Chester, PA* [8/19/00]

A: No. The ball is dead once it goes into the stands. This would be handled the same as an overthrow into the stands by a fielder. Each runner is awarded two bases from where he was at the moment the ball left the fielder's hand. A run did score on this play, much to the chagrin of the outfielder who couldn't count.

·················· **LEGAL CATCH?** ··················

Q: The batter hits a high foul fly behind the plate. The catcher forgets to take off his mask. As he looks up for the ball it comes down, hits him on the mask, bounces back into the air and he catches it in his glove. Is this a legal catch? —*Walter Smith, Chesterland, OH* [4/17/72]

A: Yes. In this case it was a good thing he forgot to take off his mask.

························· **HIDE AND GO SEEK** ·························

Q: In a Little League game, the batter bunts down the first base line. The first baseman charges the bunt and the second baseman covers first. The second baseman gets the throw, but after receiving it in plenty of time can't find the base with his foot. The runner is safe. How do you score this? —*Steve Theisen, Hudson, OH* [8/4/88]

A: Give the first baseman an assist and charge the second baseman with an error. Also, get him larger shoes.

························· **TAKE THREE** ·························

Q: Some friends and I are having a slight disagreement on a baseball problem. I say that an umpire has the right to award a ground-rule triple if he feels a batter obviously would reach third base. Please give us the full dope. —*Crawdad, Otto, Jan, and Bill, Bowling Green State University* [5/18/67]

A: You are right. If a spectator interferes with a ground ball that, in the umpire's opinion, would have been a triple, *it becomes a triple*. Rule 3.16 covers it.

························· **SCORER'S CALL** ·························

Q: If the outfielder tries to catch a deep fly but it hits his mitt and then falls out and over the fence, is this an error by the outfielder or a home run? —*Joe Adomaitis, Painesville, OH* [6/26/77]

A: This is strictly up to the scorer. If, in his judgment, the ball could have been caught with ordinary effort, he will rule it an error. If not, it's a home run.

The batter won't like the scorer if he rules it an error. And the pitcher won't like him if he doesn't. Scorers aren't always loved.

Out of Left Field

Q: It is midway in a night game, with two on and two out, when the batter lifts a rainmaker to center field. The fielder is camped under it, glasses down, glove raised, and the ball is about to drop into his hands when a strike of lightning cause a brief power failure, darkening the premises. A second flash, immediately following, shows that the ball fell safely beside the fielder who is now scrambling to find it in the hope of stopping the fielders who are now having sort of track meet. When the lights come on again the runners are gathered together near the "on deck" circle, each claiming to have circled the bases and scored during the blackout. The catcher protests that he stood at the plate all through the confusion and, he said, "Nobody passed me." Somebody had run into the home plate umpire and knocked him down so he couldn't be sure of anyone's location. After you brushed yourself off, how would you rule? —*Bob Dell, Cleveland Heights, OH* [9/21/79]

A: Very simple. It's no play and the batter returns to the plate with the previous count on him. All the runners return to their bases. And if lightning strikes twice, get the hell out of there.

TRY USING YOUR GLOVE

Q: I'm playing center field. A fly ball comes my way and I take off my cap and catch the ball in it. Is this permissible? —*Allan Friedman, Pepper Pike, OH* [10/10/98]

A: No. The batter is awarded a triple. The ball remains in play and the batter can try for home, if he wishes. But he's assured of at least three bases. It is never legal to use equipment detached from its proper place in order to deliberately touch a batter or thrown ball. Have your tried using your glove while it's on your hand?

DUG OUT

Q: Tie ball game, runner on third. Fielder makes a great catch of a foul ball, but falls into the dugout. Run scores after the catch. Is it legal? What if it was the third out? —*Harold Raines, Marion, OH* [10/15/87]

A: If it's the third out, the inning is over. But if there are fewer than two outs, the batter is out, the ball is dead and all base runners are advanced one base. Thus, the runner on third would score. The rule about going into the dugout is tricky. A fielder may go into the dugout to make a catch. After the catch, the ball remains in play. Runners can advance at their own risk. But if he catches the ball on the field and falls into the dugout, the catch is good, the ball is dead and runners are awarded one base. I never could understand why the rulemakers allowed players to go into the dugout to make a catch. Or why the ball is dead if he falls in, but not if he goes in of his own accord. If the dugout is out-of-bounds in one instance, logic dictates it should be out-of-bounds in all cases. Guess they just wanted to add a little spice to the game.

IN FLIGHT CALL

Q: Major slow-pitch game. Batter hits a long fly deep to left center. The ball is over the fielder's head and hits the fence on a fly at the 300-foot marker. It bounces off the fence, then off the fielder's chest and over the fence without touching the ground. Umpire rules "ground-rule double." I argued that it should have been a home run, since the ball never touched the ground. Was I right or was the umpire right? —*P. M. P.* [7/20/75]

A: The ump was wrong, which makes you right. It's a home run. The ball went over the fence in flight, which makes it worth four bases.

HEAVY GLOVE, HOT HAND

Q: A ball is batted fair into the outfield. The ball eludes the outfielder and rolls beyond. In pursuing the ball the outfielder intentionally drops or throws his glove off because he can run better without his glove on. Can the outfielder legally retrieve the ball without his glove under the conditions outlined? —*Joe E. Taucher, Columbus, OH* [9/17/75]

A: Absolutely. The only time there is a penalty is when a player purposely throws his glove at a batted or thrown ball *and hits it*. What you describe is perfectly legal.

The player in question must have a heavy glove or a hot hand.

······················· **Out of Left Field** ·······················

Q: Recently on the 11 o'clock news Gib Shanley told of a softball game where the batted ball struck a hawk in flight, killing the bird. The ball was caught and the umpire ruled the dead ball a base hit. I know this has come up in your column. The answer is that the bird is part of the air, therefore the ball is in play and may be caught for an out. Should Shanley have seen the error in the story or do I need to read my rule book over?
—*Gerald Goodfriend, South Euclid, OH* [7/21/81]

A: Several years ago a similar play did come up in a baseball game and at the time I went to Cal Hubbard, supervisor of American League umpires, for the answer. He said if it ever happened when he was umpiring he would rule it a catch and the batter would be out. The book, of course, doesn't cover this fowl play.

For the softball interpretation, I went to Tom Mason, the national interpreter. Here is his ruling: "This would be played the same as if the ball hit the wall. It is 'no catch,' the ball is in play. The umpire should signal and yell 'no catch.' The runner continues at his own risk."

Thus, it's a live ball and a dead bird.

························· **TAKE TWO** ·························

Q: My fraternity brothers and I have been having quite a discussion about the correct ruling on the following situations: The batter squares around as though he is going to bunt. The third baseman comes charging in, but much to his chagrin the batter pulls the bat back, swings away, and lines a shot right at him. The ball deflects off the third baseman's head and goes directly into the stands above the dugout. Home run? Ground-rule double? Is the ruling any different if an outfielder inadvertently knocks the ball into the stands in foul territory while trying to catch a fair ball near the foul line? —*Ken Peters, Denison University* [5/19/75]

A: The ruling is the same in both instances. It's a ground-rule double. Banking a double off an infielder's head is like calling your shot in billiards.

NOTHIN' DOING

Q: With the bases loaded and two outs the batter pops the first pitch weakly over the plate. The catcher doesn't need to move a step to catch the ball, but he drops it for what is an obvious error. However, the pitcher pounces on the ball and beats the lead runner to the plate for a force out that retires the side. Is the catcher credited with an assist on the play? Please answer my question. I want to be a sportswriter. —*Richard Martin* [4/23/63]

A: The catcher gets credit for nothing on this play. He can thank the pitcher for saving him from an error—and great embarrassment.

If you attain your lofty ambition, I hope the only strikes you're ever involved with are on the ball field.

PASSING A RUNNER

Q: This actually happened in a fast-pitch church league here. With one out in the bottom of the seventh—last inning—the home team is trailing by one run, but has the bases loaded with one out. The batter singles to left, scoring the runner from third easily with the tying run. The left fielder throws a strike to the catcher, who waits to tag the second runner. To avoid the tag the second runner jumps over the catcher, and in doing so kicks the ball out of the catcher's glove and tumbles past the plate without touching it. The catcher retrieves the ball and throws to the pitcher covering the plate, who tags the second runner before he can get back. But this happens after the third runner—he originally was on first—has slid safely into home. The visiting team argued that the third runner should be out for passing the second runner, and the second runner, after being tagged out, would end the inning with the score tied. The umpire ruled that the third runner scored the winning run and the game was over. You make the call. —*Tom Marquette, Ashland, OH* [10/6/83]

A: The ump was right. Only when a runner physically passes a preceding runner is he automatically out. A runner who misses a base is assumed to have touched it until the appeal is made and missed bases never affect following runners unless that missed base eventually becomes the third out. The game is over. I hope this returns peace to Ashland.

························ **UNFAIR FOUL** ························

Q: In a recent column you described a play in which the batter pops up weakly over the plate. The catcher doesn't move to make the play, but drops the ball and the pitcher retrieves it to make the out. Well, I want to know where the catcher was standing on the play. From what I can gather he must have been standing on the plate and in this case he gets a good chance of being clobbered with the bat and also an interference penalty can be called on him.

So I think in fairness to all concerned this should be called a foul ball. The umpire was wrong by not being on his toes on this particular play. But again the same old story holds true: none of us is perfect. That's why they put pencils on erasers.
—*Hank Burnosky, Canton, OH* [4/31/63]

A: The umpire wouldn't have been fair if he had called it foul, since the plate is in fair territory. He couldn't have called it "interference" because there wasn't any. He may have been on his heels but he called it right. Stay on your toes and don't throw away your pencil. You'll be right someday. As you say, none of us is perfect.

························ **AW, RAZZBERRIES** ························

Q: A ground ball is hit to the fence in left field and as the outfielder starts to throw to the infield, the ball slips from his hand and falls over the fence. How many bases does the batter get? —*Anton P.* [9/20/60]

A: Two bases. If he had already touched first at the time the ball fell over the fence, he's given third. The fielder gets an error—and razzberries.

················ **ERROR, PLAIN AND SIMPLE** ················

Q: We would like a rule concerning a foul pop fly that is dropped by a pursuing ballplayer. The player who drops the ball is charged with an error. Now if the batter is subsequently retired why should the player who dropped the ball be charged with an error? By charging the fielder with an error before the batter is retired makes it possible for a pitcher to pitch a perfect game, yet have his team charged with two, five, or, conceivably, 25 errors. Is this, then, a perfect game when he had faced and retired 27 men? —*Pooch Kubik* [3/4/67]

A: Any time the fielder makes a misplay that prolongs the life of the batter it is an error. So, by definition, if a fielder drops a foul ball he should have caught, it must be ruled an error.

Sure, it's a perfect game if a pitcher faces only 27 men and retires them in order, even though his teammates keep dropping foul balls all over the place. Errors by his teammates don't nullify the pitcher's perfection. In fact, it shows he can rise above them.

If you drop an easy pop foul that's an error, plain and simple, and subsequent events shouldn't wipe it out, I know you won't be happy with my reply, Pooch, so I expect you to bark at me.

················ **CAROM OFF A PLAYER** ················

Q: Tell this umpire he was wrong: Slow-pitch, Garfield Heights Church League. Batter hits a pop-up back of the pitcher's mound. Pitcher backs up. Ball caroms off his glove to the shortstop who juggles the ball before finally catching it *before* it hit the ground. Ump called the batter safe at first, stating when the ball hit the pitcher it was like the ball hitting a wall and the shortstop had to throw the batter out at first. —*George Jana* [8/29/76]

A: I've heard pitchers called many things but never a "wall." What you describe is a legal catch since the ball never hit the ground or any object other than a player.

Ump, you were wrong. Did I tell him, George?

·· **IT'S A HIT** ····························

Q: Man on first base. Batter grounds to the shortstop, who fields the ball cleanly, pumps to second base, then turns and throws to first. The throw is too late and the batter is safe. Is it a hit, fielder's choice or an error? —*Chuck Britton, Euclid, OH* [6/8/89]

A: Since he didn't throw to second, it has to be a base hit. The batter beat it out.

················· **ASSUMING THE DOUBLE PLAY** ·················

Q: Runner on first base, no outs. Batter grounds to short, who throws to second for the force. The second baseman's throw to first was perfect and in plenty of time to retire the batter. The first baseman dropped the ball and the ump, of course, called the batter safe. Since you aren't supposed to assume a double play, the first baseman is off the hook on this and isn't charged with an error. Right? —*Walt Smolek, Lorain, OH* [4/10/98]

A: The batter clearly would have been out at first base if the first baseman had held the ball. Hence, there is nothing to assume. It absolutely is an error by the first baseman and he should be charged with one. It is only when the pivot man, on an attempted double play, makes a wild throw to the base but there is no further advance because of it that no error is charged, even though a good throw would have resulted in a double play.

Extra Innings

You Make the Call

······················· **FAIR OR FOUL?** ·······················

A baseball often bounces funny and when it does it eventually will be foul or fair.

But whatever it is, you are certain to find someone who disagrees with the umpire's call.

We get more letters and phone calls on foul and fair balls than on any other type of play. Many fans, as well as players and managers on the sandlots, apparently are confused.

Oh, so you're not, huh? You think you know the difference between a foul ball and a fair ball?

All right. Let's see how well you do on this test. We'll give you the plays. You call 'em by underlining what you consider the correct answer.

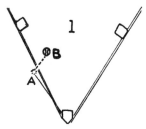

1: The ball hits in foul territory at Point A, hits a pebble and bounces into fair territory at Point B and is fielded there.
Fair or foul?
Suppose it isn't fielded at Point B, but comes to rest there.
Fair or foul?

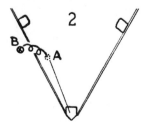

2: The ball hits at Point A in fair territory, but spins into foul territory and comes to rest or is touched at Point B.
Fair or foul?

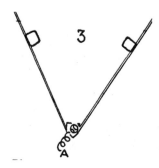

3: The ball hits at Point A in foul territory, spins forward and comes to rest directly on home plate. *Fair or foul?*

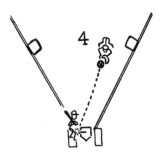

4: The ball hits the batter's leg while he is in the territory and is fielded there. *Fair or foul?*

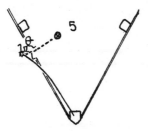

5: There is a runner taking his lead off third base in foul territory. A line drive hits him and then bounces fair, where it is fielded. *Fair or foul?*

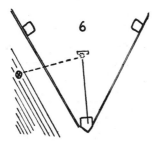

6: A line drive hits the pitcher's rubber without touching a player and caroms into foul territory between home and third and bounces into the seats. *Fair or foul?*

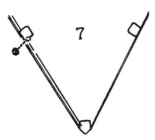

7: Ball rolls directly along the foul line, touches a corner of the base and then rolls foul, never passing the bag. *Fair or foul?*

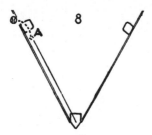

8: Ball bounces in front of the base at Point A, crosses directly over the bag and lands in foul territory beyond the bag. *Fair or foul?*

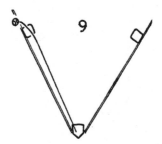

9: Line drive zooms over third base in fair territory but lands on the foul side of the left field line. *Fair or foul?*

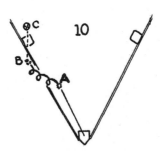

10: Ball hits fair at Point A, spins foul, hits a pebble at Point B, comes back into the diamond, crosses directly over the bag and comes to rest at Point C. *Fair or foul?*

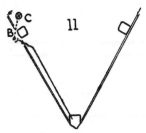

11: Ball rolls inside the line, then at Point A dips into foul territory before reaching the bag, but after it passes behind the bag, it hits a pebble at Point B and goes fair again, settling at Point C. (Don't say this is impossible. It happened on our sandlots last week.) *Fair or foul?*

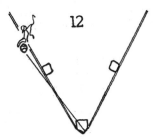

12: Third baseman standing in fair territory, reaches out into foul territory and touches a line drive which is definitely on the foul side of the line. *Fair or foul?*

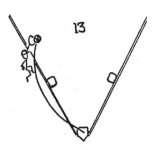

13: Left fielder goes into foul territory for long fly. At the last second the wind carries it into fair territory. While standing in foul territory, he reaches into fair territory to touch the ball. *Fair or foul?*

* * *

Time. That's enough for now.

Here are the answers: In Plays 1, 3, 7, 8, 10 and 13 it's a *Fair* ball. And of course it's *Foul* in Plays 2, 4, 5, 6, 9, 11, and 12.

Here's the definition of a fair ball: One that "settles on fair ground between home and first base, *or* between home and third base, *or* that is on or over fair territory when bounding to the out-field past first base or third base, *or* that touches first or third base, *or* that first falls on fair territory on or beyond first base or third base, *or* that, while on or over fair territory, touches the person of an umpire or player." Note: A fair or foul "fly ball shall be judged according to the position of the ball and not whether the fielder is in fair or foul territory at the time he touches it."

Conversely, a foul ball is one "that settles on foul territory between home and first base, or between home and third base, *or* that bounds past first or third base on or over foul territory, *or* that first falls on foul territory beyond first or third base, *or* that, while on or over foul territory, touches the person of the umpire, or a player or any object foreign to the natural ground."

A key word in the above definition is "settles." Thus on all calls between the play and the base it makes no difference where the ball first hits. It must be judged on where it finally comes to rest.

Also remember these two things: A pebble is part of the natural ground, just as the grass is. Also, home play is in *fair* territory.

Now how did you score on the test? If you're an umpire and got less than 100 percent, you flunked.

······················· **OVERTHROWS** ·····························

Last Sunday on these pages, we put together a quiz on the rules for baseball and softball to sharpen local sandlotters for the season. Several readers have asked for more, particularly about plays involving overthrows. "There's more confusion on this play than any other," said a manager of a softball team. "Can you clear up the rule on overthrows and this business about 'one and one'?" Here are five questions that should help.

1: Manning is on first base. Harrah flies deep to center. Manning has reached second when the ball is caught. He starts to run back to first when the center fielder throws the ball to the first baseman. The ball goes past the first baseman and out of play. The umpire awards Manning third base. *Right or wrong?*

2: Manning is on first. On a hit-and-run, Harrah singles to left. At the time of the throw to the infield, Manning is on second and Harrah has not yet reached first base. The throw goes out of play. The ump awards Manning third and Harrah second. *Right or wrong?*

3: Manning on first. Harrah grounds to deep short. Shortstop sees it's too late to get Manning, so he throws to first just before Harrah gets there. The throw goes out of play. Umpire sends Manning home and awards Harrah second base. *Right or wrong?*

4: Manning is on first. Harrah hits high fly to short right. Manning holds up between first and second and Harrah pulls up right behind him. Right fielder drops ball and throws to second trying to force Manning, but the throw is wide and, by the time Manning has rounded second, the ball goes out of play. The ump awards Manning home and Harrah third. *Right or wrong?*

5: Manning on first. Pitcher, from the rubber, tries to pick him off and throws over first baseman's head. Ball goes out of play. Ump awards Manning second. *Right or wrong?*

* * *

ANSWERS: The ump was right in Plays 1 and 5 and wrong in Plays 2, 3, and 4.

The rule on overthrows is rather simple. If the wild throw is made by an outfielder, all the runners get two bases from where they were at the time of the throw. If it is the first throw by an infielder and is made before all the runners, including the batter, have advanced safely, each is awarded two bases from where they were at the time the ball was pitched. If all of them, including the batter, had advanced at least one base at the time the infielder made the wild throw, give them two bases from where they were at the time of the throw.

There's no such thing as "one and one." Now let's apply the rule to each of the above.

1: Manning was between first and second at the time the outfielder threw the ball, which means the last base he legally occupied was first. He gets two bases beyond first. The ump correctly put him on third.

2: When the outfielder uncorked his wild throw, Manning was on second. Award him two bases, which sends him home. Since Harrah has not yet reached first, two bases would put him at second. The ump handled Harrah properly, but not Manning.

3: Since this was a first throw by an infielder, the advancement is governed by where they were at the time of the pitch. Manning was on first, so he gets third and Harrah, the batter, gets second. The ump was wrong on Manning.

4: The throw was by an outfielder, so the runners are advanced two bases from where they were at the time of the throw. Manning had not yet reached second, so his two bases would put him at third. Therefore, Harrah, who normally would be given third because he already had reached first, would have to stop at second.

5: I threw this one in to explain a special rule on pitchers' overthrows. When the pitcher's overthrow is from pitching position, each runner gets one base. But if he backs off the rubber before throwing, he becomes an infielder and each runner gets two bases. In this case, the pickoff was from the rubber, so Manning must stop at second — one base.

Hope this clears up the overthrows. Remember, umpires, there is no such animal as "one and one."

[5/11/80]

·················· **DOES THE RUN COUNT?** ··················

So you think you know baseball? Or softball?

Let's find out. Here's a fun quiz on the basic rule of the game, the scoring of runs. I constantly am asked about plays that involve the question, "Does the run count?"

Here are 10 such plays. For each one you get right, give yourself a run. For each one you miss, give me a run. The official baseball and softball rules prevail. Go ahead, beat me.

1: Indians vs. Yankees. Bases loaded, two outs. Thornton hits a home run over the fence. After all the runners have touched home, the Yankees make a legal appeal on Thornton at first base and he is called out.
    How many runs score?

2: Same bases-loaded situation. Two outs. Again Thornton hits the ball over the fence. Alexander, who was on third, misses home plate. The Yankees make a legal appeal and Alexander is called out.
    How many runs score?

3: Again the bases are loaded, two outs. Again Thornton hits one out of the park. This time Kuiper, who was on second, misses home plate. The Yankees make a legal appeal and Kuiper is called out.
    How many runs count?

4: One out, Veryzer on third, Kuiper on second. Harrah flies deep to Mickey Rivers in center. Veryzer tags up and scores after the catch. Kuiper advances, too, but leaves second base too soon. Rivers throws to second for the appeal and Kuiper is called out, which is third out.
    Does Veryzer's run count?

5: Two outs, Mickey Rivers is on third base. Wayne Garland is pitching to Graig Nettles. Garland takes a very slow windup and Rivers races home. He slides in before the pitch is on its way. Then Nettles hits the pitch and grounds out.
    Does the run count?

6: Bases loaded, two outs. Alexander hits safely to deep right center. Two runners cross the plate but Dade, who was on first, falls down, hurts his leg and is tagged out before he can get to second.
    How many runs score?

7: Bases loaded, one out. Manning hits into a double play, short to second to first, but Bonds scores before Manning is out.
    Does the run count?

8: Again bases are loaded, one out. Again Manning hits into a double play, this time to Chambliss, who steps on first and then throws to second to double Dade, sliding in. Bonds scores before Dade is out.

Does the run count?

9: Two outs, bases loaded. Manning hits a slow roller to short and the throw to second is a fraction too late to get the sliding Dade. But Dade can't hold the base and is tagged out as he overslides it. Bonds scores before Dade is out.

Does the run count?

10: Two outs, Bonds on third, Manning on first. Cox grounds to second baseman, who tries to tag Manning going to second, but misses. Now Manning is caught in a rundown between first and second and finally is tagged out. Bonds has scored long before the tag.

Does the run count?

* * *

Okay, let's see how *you* scored.

The basic rule is this: No runs can score when the third out is made by the batter before he reaches first base, or by a runner before he reaches a base he is forced to make. In all other instances the time of the third out determines whether or not the run counts.

The answers:

1: *No* runs score. Thornton never reached first base safely.

2: No runs score. Alexander never reached home, the base he had to make. Therefore, by missing home, he became a simple force-out.

3: One run counts. The runner from third legally scored, but when Kuiper became the third out by missing home, no runner behind him could score.

4: Yes, Veryzer's run counts. He scored before the third out was made and the appeal at second was *not* a forceout. It simply was a case of a runner leaving too soon.

5: No, the run doesn't count. The steal of home was all part of the same play which began when the pitcher took his position on the mound. Since the third out was recorded on the batter before he reached first, it nullified Rivers' steal.

6: No runs score. Dade was forced out at second base.

7: No runs score. The third out was made by the batter before he reached first base.

8: The run counts. When Chambliss stepped on first base the batter was out and thus the force at second was off. The run scored before the third out was recorded.

9: The run counts. Dade's out came after he reached second base.

10: No runs count. Manning had to reach second and was tagged out before he got there—a force-out.

Remember, give yourself a run for each play you got right. Give me a run for each of your wrongs.

If I beat you, don't be angry. I'm a good winner and promise to give you a makeup test some day. But I've saved up a few toughies.

[6/7/79]